Trial by Trivia I
A Trivia Poker Book Game

Table of Contents	
Questions	Pp 1-103 (Odd Pages)
Answers	Pp 2-104 (Even Pages)
Rules	Pg. 105-110
Category List	Back Cover

2ND IN THE TRIVIA POKER BOOK GAME SERIES
1ST IN THE TRIAL BY TRIVIA SERIES

Copyright © 2023 Douglas Boyle

All rights reserved. No part of this publication may be reproduced, distributed, or transmitted in any form or by any means, including photocopying, recording, or other electronic or mechanical methods, without the prior written permission of the publisher, except in the case of brief quotations embodied in critical reviews and certain other noncommercial uses permitted by copyright law.

Published by Red Bug Trivia, Casselbery FL 32707

Website: www.triviapoker.blogspot.com

CLUBS		
A♣	1	AFRICA
2♣	3	AMALGAM
3♣	5	ANCIENT HISTORY
4♣	7	ASIA
5♣	9	ASTRONOMY
6♣	11	BEVERAGES
7♣	13	BOARD GAMES
8♣	15	BOOKS
9♣	17	BUSINESS & INDUSTRY
10♣	19	COLLEGES & UNIVERSITIES
J♣	21	COOKING
Q♣	23	DESSERTS
K♣	25	DINING

DIAMONDS		
A♦	27	AFRICA
2♦	29	AMALGAM
3♦	31	ANCIENT HISTORY
4♦	33	ASIA
5♦	35	ASTRONOMY
6♦	37	BEVERAGES
7♦	39	BOARD GAMES
8♦	41	BOOKS
9♦	43	BUSINESS & INDUSTRY
10♦	45	COLLEGES & UNIVERSITIES
J♦	47	COOKING
Q♦	49	DESSERTS
K♦	51	DINING

HEARTS		
A♥	53	AFRICA
2♥	55	AMALGAM
3♥	57	ANCIENT HISTORY
4♥	59	ASIA
5♥	61	ASTRONOMY
6♥	63	BEVERAGES
7♥	65	BOARD GAMES
8♥	67	BOOKS
9♥	69	BUSINESS & INDUSTRY
10♥	71	COLLEGES & UNIVERSITIES
J♥	73	COOKING
Q♥	75	DESSERTS
K♥	77	DINING

SPADES		
A♠	79	AFRICA
2♠	81	AMALGAM
3♠	83	ANCIENT HISTORY
4♠	85	ASIA
5♠	87	ASTRONOMY
6♠	89	BEVERAGES
7♠	91	BOARD GAMES
8♠	93	BOOKS
9♠	95	BUSINESS & INDUSTRY
10♠	97	COLLEGES & UNIVERSITIES
J♠	99	COOKING
Q♠	101	DESSERTS
K♠	103	DINING

SPECIAL DRAWS

→ During Category Selection
- ◆ If you draw a previously drawn category, simply draw again

→ During Question Selection
- ◆ ACE - Selector chooses a question
- ◆ JACK - The Question switches to the rejected question, draw again
- ◆ QUEEN/KING - A Bonus card is set aside, draw Again
- ◆ LOSE A TURN - If 2 Jacks are drawn, or a Third Bonus card is drawn.

→ During Round Award Draw
- ◆ Any CLUB - Show card and draw an additional card

SCORING	
CLUBS	1
DIAMONDS	2
HEARTS	3
SPADES	4
BEST POKER HAND	10.5

TURN CHOICES
ANSWER BLUFF CHALLENGE PASS VETO

THE DECK OF PLAYING CARDS (& REINVENTING THE WHEEL)

The First Great Trivia Game was released in December of 1981, and that was Trivial Pursuit.™ It cost $39.99 that first year (it came down to $29.99 the 2nd Christmas due to economies of scale). This would cost over $90 in today's dollars. One reason why really good trivia games are rare is this cost. I made a DIY demo of this game back in 2019 and with a 50 card mock up, I spent over $50. To bring a game equivalent in style and scope to Trivial Pursuit™ in 2023 would require a price tag of around $75. To bring this game (or the other) to the public, the wheel itself had to be reinvented. There needed to be a way to do this affordably. No idea was off the table, and this was worked on for 5 years. The challenge was to do this for under $30.

The largest cost in a trivia game is the packs of Trivia cards. Each card is a separate template and they would account for more than 70% of the cost of production (even more in smaller batches). The first "Eureka" moment was the realization that listing the questions in a book-style format would cut this cost by about 1/6th. And a book is elegant, familiar, and very functional (and with the ebook option even more affordable).

The next two biggest costs (at around 10% each) are the games packaging and game board. The Book format also streamlines the packaging issue, but what about the game board?

The idea then became what if we sell a board game without a game board, but direct people to use things they already had? Maybe you could move tokens on a checkerboard? What is a game board except a method for tallying points earned? Maybe they could move quarters along a 30 day calendar?

The 2nd "Eureka" moment was when it was decided to run the scoring via standard playing cards. A 2019 poll stated that 70% of US households own a deck of playing cards. They are given away at conventions and hotels. Even if you don't have one, you can buy one on Amazon for about 5 bucks. Also the cards can both serve as the scoring mechanism and the randomization mechanism simultaneously. And Poker is familiar to most people, we didn't have to reinvent the wheel a second time. This is how the format for these trivia games was born, which miraculously allowed production to be cheaper than what it was in 1981, while still producing a challenging and fun game. You can purchase a great game at an unbelievably great price. This version beat the goal price by 50%+

AFRICA A♣

A	Choose a Question
2	In 2022, an African Country had the best finish at the World Cup of any African nation. Name the 13 African Countries that have qualified for Soccer's premier tournament
3	In terms of nominal gross GDP, Ghana is the 13th most productive Africa country (2022 estimates). Name the 12 biggest current economies in Africa
4	Yaounde, Cameroon has about half a million more people than Los Angeles and ranks as the 14th most populous African City. Name the 13 largest African cities by population
5	Africa is home to approximately 12% of the World's Oil Reserves, producing nearly 5 billion barrels per day. Name the top 10 top African Oil-producing countries.
6	12 African countries are larger than 1 Million square Kilometers. Name the 12 largest African Countries by Area
7	South Africa became Independent first in 1910. The most recent African Country to gain Independence was in 2011. Name the 10 foreign Nations from which the mainland African Countries have declared Independence
8	Between Morocco to the North and South Africa to the South, 20 other mainland countries have Atlantic Ocean coastline. Name any of these coastal countries.
9	The Nile River and its drainage basin flows through or along 11 countries. Name them
10	Of the African Nations that are full members of the United Nations, 14 of them have an English Official name that ends in a consonant. Name them.

AFRICA A♣

2
1. Cameroon
2. Morocco
3. Nigeria
4. Tunisia
5. Ghana
6. Algeria
7. Senegal
8. Egypt
9. South Africa
10. Ivory Coast
11. D.R. Congo
12. Angola
13. Togo

3
1. Nigeria
2. Egypt
3. South Africa
4. Algeria
5. Morocco
6. Angola
7. Kenya
8. Ethiopia
9. Tanzania
10. Ghana
11. Ivory Coast
12. D.R. Congo

4
1. Cairo, Egypt
2. Kinshasa, DR Congo
3. Lagos, Nigeria
4. Giza, Egypt
5. Luanda, Angola
6. Dar es Salaam, Tanzania
7. Khartoum, Sudan
8. Johannesburg, South Africa
9. Abidjan, Cote D'Ivoire
10. Alexandria, Egypt
11. Addis Ababa, Ethiopia
12. Nairobi, Kenya
13. Cape Town, South Africa

5
1. Angola
2. Nigeria
3. Algeria
4. Libya
5. Egypt
6. Congo
7. Gabon
8. Ghana
9. Equatorial Guinea
10. Chad

6
1. Algeria
2. DR Congo
3. Sudan
4. Libya
5. Chad
6. Niger
7. Angola
8. Mali
9. South Africa
10. Ethiopia
11. Mauritania
12. Egypt

7
1. Great Britain
2. France
3. Spain
4. Portugal
5. Belgium
6. Italy
7. Egypt (Sudan)
8. Sudan (South Sudan)
9. Ethiopia (Eritrea)
10. Namibia (South Africa)

8
1. Angola
2. Benin
3. Cameroon
4. DR Congo
5. Equatorial Guinea
6. Gabon
7. Gambia
8. Guinea-Bissau
9. Ivory Coast
10. Liberia
11. Libya
12. Mauritania
13. Morocco
14. Namibia
15. Nigeria
16. Congo
17. Senegal
18. Sierra Leone
19. Togo
20. Tunisia

9
1. DR Congo
2. Tanzania
3. Burundi
4. Rwanda
5. Uganda
6. Kenya
7. Ethiopia
8. Eritrea
9. South Sudan
10. Sudan
11. Egypt

10
1. Benin
2. Gabon
3. Niger
4. Senegal
5. Seychelles
6. Cameroon
7. Central African Republic
8. Chad
9. Comoros
10. South Sudan
11. Sudan
12. Madagascar
13. Egypt
14. Mauritius

AMALGAM 2♣

A	Choose a Question

2	SNL's Celebrity Jeopardy skit ran 15 times with Darrell Hammond & Will Ferrell in all 15, Norm McDonald and Jimmy Fallon were in the next most with 6. Name any of the 11 Celebrities these 4 impersonated.

3	The Beatles have sold more records than any Group in History, likely more than half a billion. 17 other groups (not individuals) can claim record sales of greater than 100 million copies. Name any of these 17 groups.

4	If you correctly place your hands on the letters of the home row of a typewriter or keyboard, the two index fingers are tasked with covering 6 letters each. Name these 12 letters

5	There are 15 countries or Empires who have, at their peak in square miles, controlled area larger than Nazi Germany at its peak. Name History's 15 largest Empires or Countries in Area.

6	Columbus Day, which is now often celebrated as Indigenous Peoples' Day is one of 11 U.S. Federal Holidays. Name the other 10

7	10 US Metro Areas, according to the 2020 US Census, have a Jewish population greater than 100,000 people. 2 other cities are in the 90-100K range. Name any of the 12 US Cities with the largest Jewish population.

8	*As of Fall 2023, Taylor Swift has had 10 Billboard #1 hits, as well as 8 Billboard #2s. Name any of these chart-topping Taylor Swift songs.*

9	A 2022 Lombardo Homes commissioned poll, Americans identified the Household chores they hate the most. Preparing Meals was listed #14. Name any of the 13 Household chores Americans dislike more.

10	The 20 most populous cities in the USA are located in 13 US States. Name any of the 13 states that contain the most populated cities in the USA.

Amalgam 2♣

2
1. Alex Trebek (Farrell)
2. Sean Connery (Hammond)
3. Phil Donahue (Hammond)
4. John Travolta (Hammond)
5. Burt Reynolds (MacDonald)
6. Adam Sandler (Fallon)
7. Nicolas Cage (Fallon)
8. French Stewart (Fallon)
9. Hilary Swank (Fallon)
10. Robin WIlliams (Fallon)
11. Dave Matthews (Fallon)

3
1. Queen
2. Led Zeppelin
3. Pink Floyd
4. Eagles
5. AC/DC
6. Rolling Stones
7. U2
8. Aerosmith
9. ABBA
10. Metallica
11. Maroon 5
12. Red Hot Chili Peppers
13. Fleetwood Mac
14. Bon Jovi
15. Bee Gees
16. Coldplay
17. Linkin Park

4
1. B
2. F
3. G
4. H
5. J
6. M
7. N
8. R
9. T
10. U
11. V
12. Y

5
1. British Empire
2. Mongol Empire
3. Russian Empire
4. China
5. Spanish Empire
6. French Empire
7. Umayyad Caliphate
8. Canada
9. United States of America
10. Brazil
11. Australia
12. Persian
13. Portuguese
14. Empire of Japan
15. Ottoman Empire

6
1. New Year's Day
2. Martin Luther King, Jr Day
3. President's Day
4. Memorial Day
5. Juneteenth
6. Independence Day
7. Labor Day
8. Veterans Day
9. Thanksgiving Day
10. Christmas

7
1. New York
2. Los Angeles
3. Philadelphia
4. Chicago
5. Washington DC
6. Boston
7. San Francisco
8. Atlanta
9. Baltimore
10. San Diego
11. Phoenix
12. Denver

8
1. You Belong With Me
2. Today Was a Fairytale
3. We Are Never Ever Getting Back Together
4. I Knew You Were Trouble
5. Shake it Off
6. Blank Space
7. Bad Blood
8. I Don't Wanna Live Forever
9. Look at What you Made me Do
10. Me!
11. You Need to Calm down
12. Cardigan
13. Willow
14. Anti-Hero
15. Lavender Haze
16. Karma
17. Cruel Summer
18. Is It Over Now?

9
1. Cleaning Bathroom
2. Washing Dishes
3. Doing Laundry
4. Cleaning Refrigerator
5. Yard Work/Lawn Mowing
6. Sweeping Floors
7. Dusting
8. Cleaning the Kitchen
9. Organizing/picking up Clutter
10. Taking out Trash
11. Washing Windows
12. Vacuuming
13. Cleaning the Garage

10
1. New York
2. California
3. Illinois
4. Texas
5. Arizona
6. Pennsylvania
7. Florida
8. Ohio
9. North Carolina
10. Indiana
11. Washington
12. Colorado
13. Oklahoma

ANCIENT HISTORY 3♣

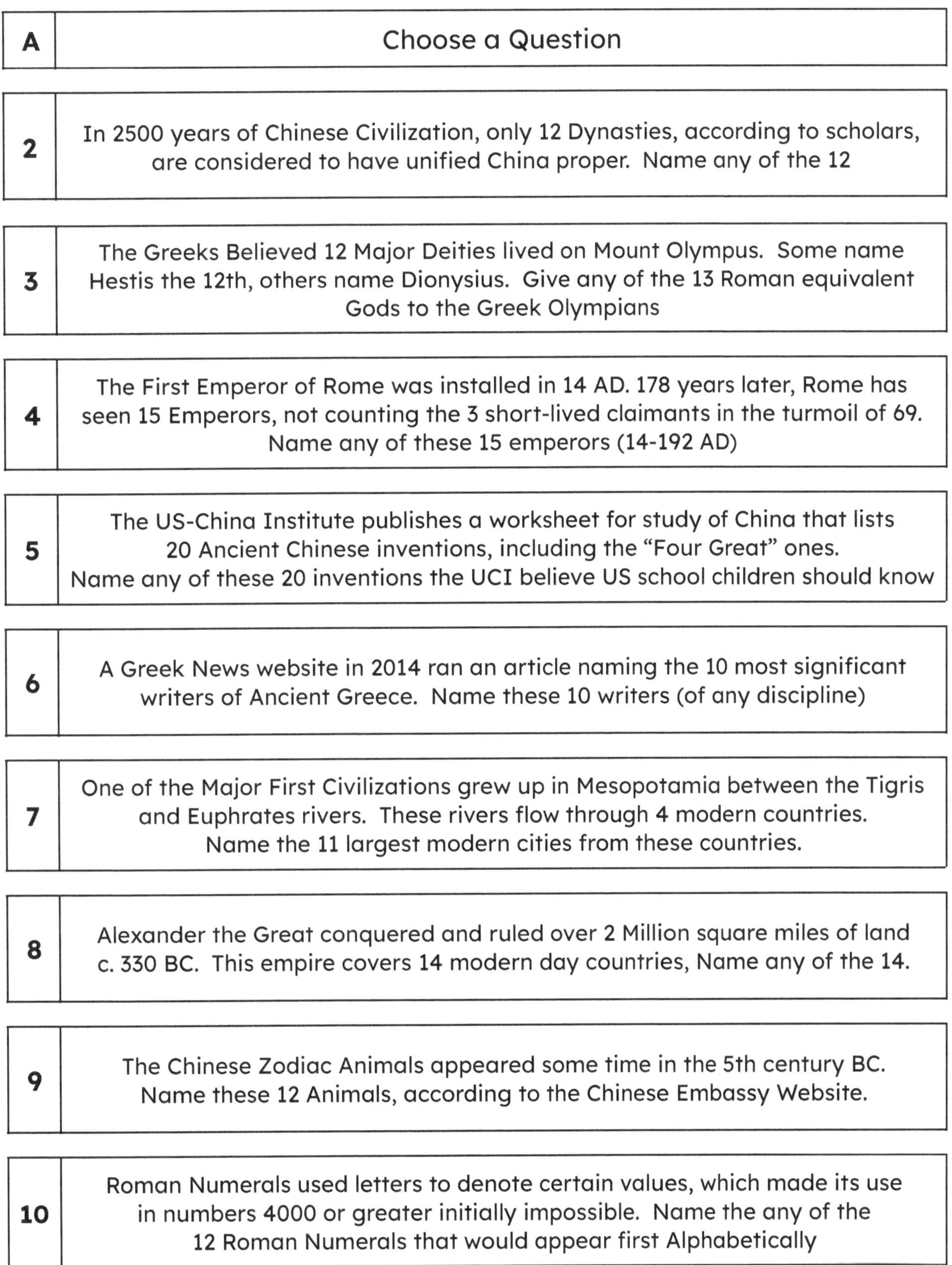

A	Choose a Question
2	In 2500 years of Chinese Civilization, only 12 Dynasties, according to scholars, are considered to have unified China proper. Name any of the 12
3	The Greeks Believed 12 Major Deities lived on Mount Olympus. Some name Hestis the 12th, others name Dionysius. Give any of the 13 Roman equivalent Gods to the Greek Olympians
4	The First Emperor of Rome was installed in 14 AD. 178 years later, Rome has seen 15 Emperors, not counting the 3 short-lived claimants in the turmoil of 69. Name any of these 15 emperors (14-192 AD)
5	The US-China Institute publishes a worksheet for study of China that lists 20 Ancient Chinese inventions, including the "Four Great" ones. Name any of these 20 inventions the UCI believe US school children should know
6	A Greek News website in 2014 ran an article naming the 10 most significant writers of Ancient Greece. Name these 10 writers (of any discipline)
7	One of the Major First Civilizations grew up in Mesopotamia between the Tigris and Euphrates rivers. These rivers flow through 4 modern countries. Name the 11 largest modern cities from these countries.
8	Alexander the Great conquered and ruled over 2 Million square miles of land c. 330 BC. This empire covers 14 modern day countries, Name any of the 14.
9	The Chinese Zodiac Animals appeared some time in the 5th century BC. Name these 12 Animals, according to the Chinese Embassy Website.
10	Roman Numerals used letters to denote certain values, which made its use in numbers 4000 or greater initially impossible. Name the any of the 12 Roman Numerals that would appear first Alphabetically

Ancient History 3♣

2
1. Qin
2. Western Han
3. Xin
4. Eastern Han
5. Western Jin
6. Sui
7. Tang
8. Wu Zhou
9. Northern Song
10. Yuan
11. Ming
12. Qing

3
1. Jupiter
2. Juno
3. Neptune
4. Ceres
5. Minerva
6. Apollo
7. Diana
8. Mars
9. Venus
10. Vulcan
11. Mercury
12. Vesta
13. Bacchu

4
1. Augustus
2. Tiberius
3. Caligula
4. Claudius
5. Nero
6. Vespasian
7. Titus
8. Domitian
9. Nerva
10. Trajan
11. Hadrian
12. Anotninus Pius
13. Marcus Aurelius
14. Lucius Verus
15. Commodus

5
1. Paper making
2. Movable Type
3. Gunpowder
4. Compass
5. Alcohol
6. Mechanical Clock
7. Tea
8. Silk
9. Umbrella
10. Acupuncture
11. Iron Smelting
12. Porcelain
13. Earthquake Detector
14. Rocket
15. Bronze
16. The Kite
17. The Seed Drill
18. Row Crop Farming
19. Toothbrush
20. Paper Money

6
1. Homer
2. Sophocles
3. Herodotus
4. Euripides
5. Hippocrates
6. Aristophanes
7. Plato
8. Aristotle
9. Euclid
10. Archimedes

7
1. Baghdad, Iraq
2. Mosul, Iraq
3. Basra, Iraq
4. Nasiriyah, Iraq
5. Hillah, Iraq
6. Sulaymaniyah, Iraq
7. Tehran, Iran
8. Mashhad, Iran
9. Aleppo, Syria
10. Istanbul, Turkey
11. Ankara, Turkey

8
1. Greece
2. Albania
3. Bulgaria
4. North Macedonia
5. Turkey
6. Iran
7. Iraq
8. Kuwait
9. Syria
10. Jordan
11. Israel
12. Pakistan
13. Afghanistan
14. Tajikistan

9
1. Rat
2. Ox
3. Tiger
4. Rabbit
5. Dragon
6. Snake
7. Horse
8. Goat
9. Monkey
10. Rooster
11. Dog
12. Pig

10
1. 100 (C)
2. 200 (CC)
3. 300 (CCC)
4. 301 (CCCI)
5. 302 (CCCII)
6. 303 (CCCIII)
7. 309 (CCCIX)
8. 390 (CCCXC)
9. 391 (CCCXCI)
10. 392 (CCCXCII)
11. 393 (CCCXCIII)
12. 399 (CCCXCIX

Asia 4♣

A	Choose a Question

2	China shares a border with 14 countries. Name them

3	18 of the 48 countries in Asia have National flags that have the color Green in it. The Greenish color on the Sri Lankan Flag is officially Teal, so it's not on this list. Name Any of the 18 countries with Green on their Flag.

4	US News' list of the 15 best places to visit in Asia includes 11 cities, 1 Island country, 3 regions, and one dramatic geographic feature. Name any of these 15 locations

5	13 of the 20 largest cities (by Metro Population) lie in Asia, and have at least 13 million residents. Name any of the 13 most populous Asian Cities.

6	14 mainland Asian countries have coast along the Indian Ocean, counting bays, seas, and inlets. Name any of these 14 Asian Nations.

7	13 of the remaining world monarchies are located in the Asian Continent, calling their leader either King, Sultan, Agong, Emir, or Emperor. Name these 13 nations with Monarchies

8	11 countries in Asia have a GDP per capita of over $20,000 (in US Dollars). Name the wealthiest 11 Asian Countries

9	The United Arab Emirates (UAE) joined the United Nations in 1971. Since then 12 other Asian Nations have become members over the past 50 years. Name the newest 12 Asian Members of the U.N.

10	On the continent of Asia, 11 countries do not have direct access to an ocean. Name these 11 land-locked countries

ASIA 4♣

2
1. Afghanistan
2. Bhutan
3. India
4. Kazakhstan
5. North Korea
6. Kyrgyzstan
7. Laos
8. Mongolia
9. Myanmar
10. Nepal
11. Pakistan
12. Russia
13. Tajikistan
14. Vietnam

3
1. Azerbaijan
2. Bangladesh
3. India
4. Iran
5. Iraq
6. Jordan
7. Kuwait
8. Lebanon
9. Maldives
10. Myanmar
11. Oman
12. Pakistan
13. Saudi Arabia
14. Syria
15. Tajikistan
16. Turkmenistan
17. Uzbekistan
18. UAE

4
1. Tokyo, Japan
2. Maldives
3. Phuket, Thailand
4. Sagarmatha National Park (Mt.Everest-Nepal)
5. Hong Kong
6. Chiang Mai, Thailand
7. Bali, Indonesia
8. Bangkok, Thailand
9. Kyoto, Japan
10. Singapore
11. Jaipur, India
12. Hanoi Vietnam
13. Railay Beach< Thailand
14. Taipei, Taiwan
15. Seoul, South Korea

5
1. Tokyo, Japan
2. Delhi, India
3. Shanghai, China
4. Mumbai, India
5. Beijing, China
6. Dhaka, Bangladesh
7. Osaka, Japan
8. Karachi, Pakistan
9. Chongqing, China
10. Istanbul, Turkey
11. Kolkata, India
12. Manila, Philippines
13. Tianjin, China

6
1. Bangladesh
2. India
3. Iran
4. Iraq
5. Israel
6. Jordan
7. Myanmar
8. Oman
9. Pakistan
10. Qatae
11. Saudi Arabia
12. Thailand
13. UAE
14. Yemen

7
1. Bahrain
2. Bhutan
3. Brunei
4. Cambodia
5. Japan
6. Jordan
7. Kuwait
8. Malaysia
9. Oman
10. Qatar
11. Saudi Arabia
12. Thailand
13. UAE

8
1. Singapore
2. Qatar
3. Israel
4. Japan
5. Saudi Arabia
6. UAE
7. South Korea
8. Taiwan
9. Brunei
10. Bahrain
11. Kuwait

9
1. Timor-Leste
2. Uzbekistan
3. Turkmenistan
4. Tajikistan
5. Kyrgyzstan
6. Kazakhstan
7. Azerbaijan
8. Armenia
9. South Korea
10. Brunei
11. Vietnam
12. Bangladesh

10
1. Uzbekistan
2. Turkmenistan
3. Tajikistan
4. Nepal
5. Mongolia
6. Kazakhstan
7. Laos
8. Bhutan
9. Azerbaijan
10. Armenia
11. Afghanistan

Astronomy 5♣

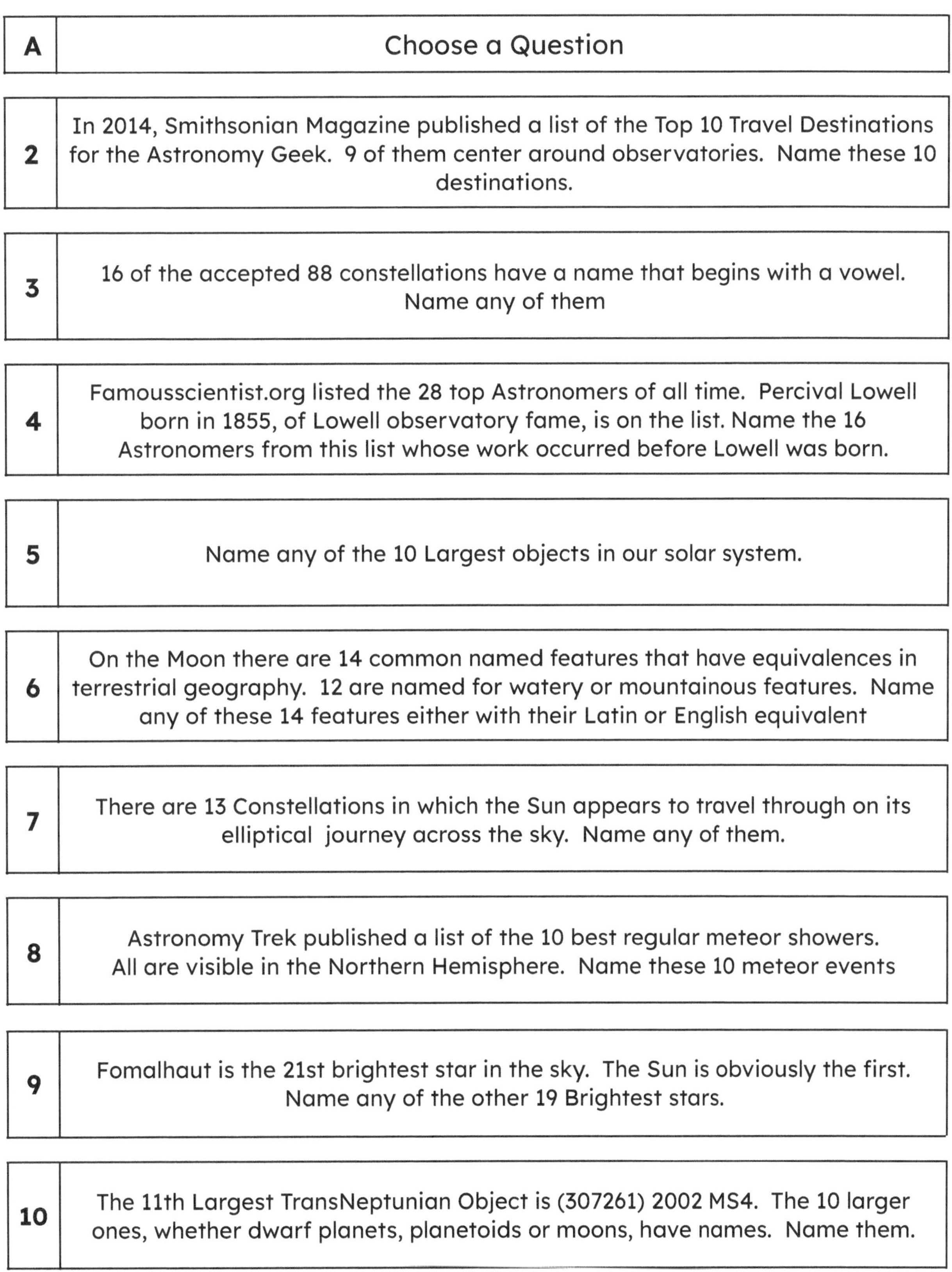

A	Choose a Question
2	In 2014, Smithsonian Magazine published a list of the Top 10 Travel Destinations for the Astronomy Geek. 9 of them center around observatories. Name these 10 destinations.
3	16 of the accepted 88 constellations have a name that begins with a vowel. Name any of them
4	Famousscientist.org listed the 28 top Astronomers of all time. Percival Lowell born in 1855, of Lowell observatory fame, is on the list. Name the 16 Astronomers from this list whose work occurred before Lowell was born.
5	Name any of the 10 Largest objects in our solar system.
6	On the Moon there are 14 common named features that have equivalences in terrestrial geography. 12 are named for watery or mountainous features. Name any of these 14 features either with their Latin or English equivalent
7	There are 13 Constellations in which the Sun appears to travel through on its elliptical journey across the sky. Name any of them.
8	Astronomy Trek published a list of the 10 best regular meteor showers. All are visible in the Northern Hemisphere. Name these 10 meteor events
9	Fomalhaut is the 21st brightest star in the sky. The Sun is obviously the first. Name any of the other 19 Brightest stars.
10	The 11th Largest TransNeptunian Object is (307261) 2002 MS4. The 10 larger ones, whether dwarf planets, planetoids or moons, have names. Name them.

Astronomy 5♣

2
1. Mauna Kea Observatory (Hawaii)
2. Very Large Array (New Mexico)
3. Royal Observatory Greenwich (London U.K.)
4. Cerro Paranal (Chile)
5. Kitt Peak National Observatory (Arizona)
6. Griffith Observatory (Los Angeles)
7. South African Astronomical Observatory (Sutherland)
8. Arcetri Astrophysical Observatory (Italy)
9. Teide National Park (Canary Islands, Spain)
10. Hayden Planetarium (New York)

3
1. Sirius
2. Canopus
3. Rigil Kentaurus A
4. Rigil Kentaurus B
5. Arcturus
6. Vega
7. Capella
8. Rigel
9. Procyon
10. Achernar
11. Hadar
12. Betelgeuse
13. Altair
14. Acrux A
15. Acrux B
16. Aldebaran
17. Antares
18. Spica
19. Pollux

4
1. Anaximander
2. Aristarchus
3. Tyco Brahe
4. Nicolaus Copernicus
5. Democritus
6. Eudoxus
7. Galileo Galilei
8. Carl Friedrich Gauss
9. Thomas Herriot
10. Caroline Herschel
11. John Herschel
12. Hipparchus
13. Omar Khayyam
14. John Mitchell
15. Isaac Newton
16. Claudius Ptolemy

5
1. Sun
2. Jupiter
3. Saturn
4. Uranus
5. Neptune
6. Earth
7. Venus
8. Mars
9. Ganymede (Moon of Jupiter)
10. Titan (Moon of Saturn)

6
1. Maria (Seas)
2. Oceanus (Oceans)
3. Lacus (Lakes)
4. Sinus (Bays)
5. Paludes (Marshes)
6. Catenae (Craters)
7. Vallis (Valleys)
8. Mons (Mountains)
9. Dorsa (Ridges)
10. Promontoria (Capes)
11. Rimae (Channels/Rivers)
12. Rupes (Cliffs)
13. Terrae (Continents)

7
1. Aries
2. Aquarius
3. Cancer
4. Capricorn
5. Gemini
6. Leo
7. Libra
8. Ophiuchus
9. Pisces
10. Sagittarius
11. Scorpio
12. Taurus
13. Virgo

8
1. Quadrantids
2. Lyrids
3. Eta Aquarids
4. Capricornids
5. Perseids
6. Orionids
7. Taurids
8. Leonids
9. Geminids
10. Ursids

9
1. Ara
2. Aries
3. Auriga
4. Equuleus
5. Eridanus
6. Indus
7. Octans
8. Ophiuchus
9. Orion
10. Ursa Major
11. Ursa Minor

10
1. Pluto
2. Eris
3. Haumea
4. Makemake
5. Gonggong
6. Charon (Moon-Pluto)
7. Quaoar
8. Sedna
9. Orcus
10. Salacia

BEVERAGES 6♣

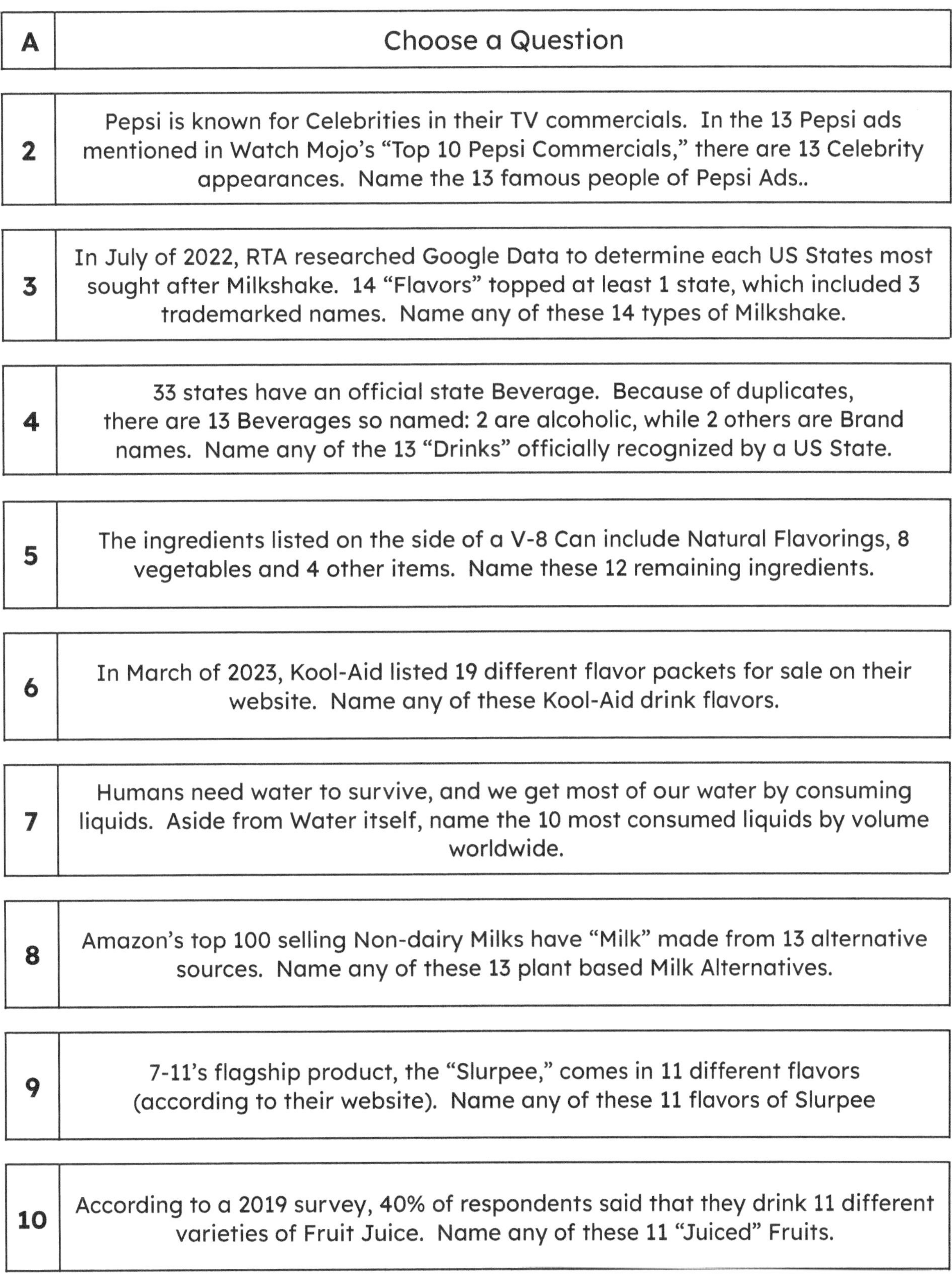

A	Choose a Question
2	Pepsi is known for Celebrities in their TV commercials. In the 13 Pepsi ads mentioned in Watch Mojo's "Top 10 Pepsi Commercials," there are 13 Celebrity appearances. Name the 13 famous people of Pepsi Ads..
3	In July of 2022, RTA researched Google Data to determine each US States most sought after Milkshake. 14 "Flavors" topped at least 1 state, which included 3 trademarked names. Name any of these 14 types of Milkshake.
4	33 states have an official state Beverage. Because of duplicates, there are 13 Beverages so named: 2 are alcoholic, while 2 others are Brand names. Name any of the 13 "Drinks" officially recognized by a US State.
5	The ingredients listed on the side of a V-8 Can include Natural Flavorings, 8 vegetables and 4 other items. Name these 12 remaining ingredients.
6	In March of 2023, Kool-Aid listed 19 different flavor packets for sale on their website. Name any of these Kool-Aid drink flavors.
7	Humans need water to survive, and we get most of our water by consuming liquids. Aside from Water itself, name the 10 most consumed liquids by volume worldwide.
8	Amazon's top 100 selling Non-dairy Milks have "Milk" made from 13 alternative sources. Name any of these 13 plant based Milk Alternatives.
9	7-11's flagship product, the "Slurpee," comes in 11 different flavors (according to their website). Name any of these 11 flavors of Slurpee
10	According to a 2019 survey, 40% of respondents said that they drink 11 different varieties of Fruit Juice. Name any of these 11 "Juiced" Fruits.

BEVERAGES 6♣

2
1. Britney Spears
2. Shakira
3. Michael J Fox
4. Beyonce
5. Erique Iglesias
6. Pink
7. Madonna
8. Cindy Crawford
9. Michael Jackson
10. Alfonso Ribeiro
11. Ray Charles
12. Kylie Minogue
13. Robert Palmer

3
1. Strawberry
2. Chocolate
3. Oreo
4. Shamrock
5. Vanilla
6. Chocolate Malted
7. Coffee
8. Banana
9. Orange Creamsicle
10. Pineapple
11. Nutella
12. Peach
13. Peanut Butter
14. Peppermint

4
1. Moonshine (AL)
2. Rye Whiskey (VA
3. Milk
4. Coffee
   Flavored Milk
5. Tea
6. Lemonade
7. Tomato Juice
8. Apple Cider
9. Cranberry Juice
10. Orange Juice
11. Kool-Aid
12. Moxie
13. Kava (Awa)

5
1. Water
2. Tomato
3. Carrot
4. Celery
5. Beets
6. Parsley
7. Lettuce
8. Watercress
9. Spinach
10. Salt
11. Ascorbic Acid (Vitamin C)
12. Citric Acid

6
1. Tropical Punch
2. Cherry
3. Pink Lemonade
4. Strawberry Kiwi
5. Orand
6. Black Cherry
7. Aguas Frescas Jamaica
8. Lemon-Lime
9. Aguas Frescas Mandarina
10. Berry Cherry
11. Lemonade
12. Strawberry
13. Grape
14. Blue Raspberry
15. Aguas Frescas Pineapple
16. Mixed Berry
17. Sharkleberry
18. Aguas Frescas Mango
19. Strawberry Lemonade

7
1. Tea
2. Coffee
3. Orange Juice
4. Beer
5. Coca Cola
6. Wine
7. Vodka
8. Energy Drinks
9. Soup
10. Breast Milk

8
1. Oats
2. Almonds
3. Macadamia
4. Soybean
5. Coconut
6. Pea
7. Hemp
8. Flax
9. Rice
10. Cashew
11. Boba/Tapioca/Cassava
    Root
12. Mushroom
13. Bananas

9
1. Cherry
2. Coke
3. Blue Raspberry
4. Pina Colada
5. Dragon Fruit
6. Mango Lemonade
7. Dr Pepper
8. Peach
9. Sprite Lymonade
10. Hibiscus Lemonade
11. Summertime Citrus

10
1. Apple
2. Orange
3. Strawberry
4. Grape
5. Pineapple
6. Mango
7. Cranberry
8. Cherry
9. Lemon
10. Peach
11. Watermelon

BOARD GAMES 7♣

A	Choose a Question

2	In the game of Monopoly, there are 10 named squares you can land on that aren't properties nor railroads. Name them.

3	Hasbro updated the 1943 game Clue to have it set in a Modern Mansion in 2008. 4 Weapons and 7 rooms were changed. Name any of these 11 items that were in the original game but not in the 2008 version

4	In the game of Risk there are 42 countries, only 16 of which share their names with current countries. Name these countries

5	The 1995 board game Settlers of Catan utilizes 6 resources. The 1904 game of Pit has 7 original commodities. Name any of these 13 items.

6	Cardinal Games makes the 12 in 1 Wooden Classic Games Box Set. Name the 12 games it says are included on the packaging.

7	In the game of Operation, one plays as a surgeon gaining money for removing items to "cure" 13 ailments. Name the items removed

8	The Game of Life had 7 career paths in its' first edition, while the game Careers had 9. 3 of these overlapped. Aside from the 2 rather nebulously named Space & Superstar, Name the other 11 occupations available in these 2 games.

9	In the battle game of Stratego, each side starts with 40 pieces of 12 different ranks. Name these 12 ranks.

10	Among the tiles in the game of Scrabble, 11 letters have values that are even numbers. Name them

BOARD GAMES 7♣

2
1. Go
2. Community Chest
3. Income Tax
4. Chance
5. Jail
6. Electric Company
7. Free Parking
8. Water Works
9. Go to Jail
10. Luxury Tax

3
1. Ballroom
2. Conservatory
3. Billiard Room
4. Library
5. Cellar
6. Lounge
7. Study
8. Knife
9. Pistol
10. Lead Pipe
11. Wrench

4
1. Venezuela
2. Argentina
3. Peru
4. Brazil
5. Iceland
6. Great Britain
7. Ukraine
8. Egypt
9. Congo
10. South Africa
11. Madagascar
12. Afghanistan
13. Mongolia
14. China
15. India
16. Indonesia

5
1. Flax
2. Hay
3. Oats
4. Rye
5. Corn
6. Barley
7. Wheat
8. Brick
9. Lumber
10. Wool
11. Grain
12. Gold

6
1. CHeckers
2. Chess
3. Parcheesi
4. Chinese Checkers
5. Mancala
6. Pass Out
7. Backgammon
8. Snakes and Ladders
9. Tic Tac Toe
10. Playing Cards
11. Solitaire
12. Pick Up Sticks

7
1. Adam's Apple
2. Broken Heart
3. Wrenched Ankle
4. Butterflies in Stomach
5. Spare Ribs
6. Water on the Knee
7. Funny Bone
8. Charlie Horse
9. Writer's Cramp
10. Ankle Bone connected to Knee Bone
11. Wish Bone
12. Brain Freeze
13. Bread Basket

8
1. Athlete/Sports
2. Artist/The Arts
3. Teacher/Teaching
4. Ecology (Scientist)
5. Big Business (Businessman)
6. Politics (Politician)r
7. Travel Agent
8. Doctor
9. Sales Person
10. Accountant
11. Police Officer

9
1. Marshal
2. General
3. Colonel
4. Major
5. Captain
6. Lieutenant
7. Sergeant
8. Miner
9. Scout
10. Spy
11. Bomb
12. Flag

10
1. D
2. G
3. F
4. H
5. V
6. W
7. Y
8. J
9. X
10. Q
11. Z

Books 8♣

A	Choose a Question

2	Harry Potter and the Chamber of Secrets is the 12th best selling fiction book of all-time. Name the 11 Books that sold more.

3	13 Books or series of Books account for the Top 40 Box Office Movie Adaptations. Ready Player One just misses at #41. Name these 13 Books or Book Series

4	.WordsRated Surveyed 76,000 Americans to find out America's Favorite Book. The Harry Potter series came in 3rd. Name the 15 individual other books that ranked 1 through 16.

5	According to the Free Dictionary, there are 13 compound words in the English language that are either 9 or 10 letters long ending in -book. Name them

6	In 1995, the Mystery Writers of America published a book detailing "The Top 100 Mystery Novels of All Time." 13 authors had books in the top 15 Name these 13 remarkable Mystery authors.

7	The Best-Selling Dictionaries on Amazon include many of the other-language-to-English Variety. 10 Languages appear in the Top 100. Name the Languages Represented.

8	The Star Wars & Peter Rabbit series of books have sold an estimated 150 million copies placing them in a tie for 13th in number of books sold by series. Name the 12 series of books that sold more

9	The Ohio State University is #13 on the list of American Colleges Research Libraries measured by volume of books (2020). The top 12 all have more than 10 Million Volumes. Name these US Schools

10	U.S. Presidents often publish Autobiographies. 10 of them did so before becoming President. Name these Presidential Authors

Books 8♣

2
1. Don Quixote (Cervantes)
2. A Tale of Two Cities (Dickens)
3. The Little Prince (de Saint-Exupery)
4. Harry Potter and the Philosopher's Stone (Rowling)
5. And Then There Were None (Christie)
6. Dream of the Red Chamber (Xueqin)
7. The Hobbit (Tolkein)
8. The Lion the Witch and the Wardrobe (Lewis)
9. She: A History of Adventure (Haggard)
10. Vardi Wala Gunda (Sharma)
11. The Da Vinci Code (Brown)

3
1. Harry Potter Series
2. Hunger Games Series
3. Twilight Series
4. Jurassic Park Series
5. Alice In Wonderland (Disney)
6. The Chronicles of Narnia: The Lion, The Witch and the Wardrobe.
7. How the Grinch Stole Christmas (Dr Seuss Books)
8. Shrek! Series
9. The Da Vinci Code
10. Charlie and the Chocolate Factory
11. The Polar Express
12. The Firm
13. Divergent
14. Stuart Little

4
1. Pride and Prejudice
2. To Kill a Mockingbird
3. Where the Crawdads Sing
4. The Lord of the Rings
5. The Great Gatsby
6. The Alchemist
7. Jane Eyre
8. Verity
9. It Ends With Us
10. The Stand
11. Outlander
12. The Book Thief
13. Nightingale
14. Little Women
15. Gone With The Wind

5
1. Guidebook
2. scrapbook
3. stylebook
4. checkbook
5. storybook
6. psalmbook
7. audiobook
8. matchbook
9. sourcebook
10. schoolbook
11. pocketbook
12. promptbook
13. sketchbook

6
1. Agatha Christie
2. Arthur Conan Doyle
3. Dashiell Hammett
4. John Le Carre
5. Truman Capote
6. Harper Lee
7. Josephine Tey
8. Gregory McDonald
9. Daphne du Maurier
10. Mario Puzo
11. Umberto Eco
12. Fyodor Dostoevsky
13. Raymond Chandler

7
1. Spanish
2. French
3. Italian
4. German
5. American Sign Language
6. Arabic
7. Russian
8. Latin
9. Japanese
10. Hebrew

8
1. Harry Potter (Rowling)
2. Goosebumps (Stein)
3. Perry Mason(Gardner)
4. Berenstain Bears (Berenstain)
5. Choose You Own Adventure (Various)
6. Sweet Valley High (Pascal)
7. Noddy (Blyton)
8. Nancy Drew (Keene)
9. Thomas the Tank Engine (Awdry)
10. San Antonio (Dard)
11. Robert Langdon (Brown)
12. Babysitters Club (Martin)

9
1. Harvard
2. University of Michigan
3. Yale
4. University of Illinois
5. Columbia
6. University ofCalifornia-Los Angeles (UCLA)
7. University of California, Berkeley
8. University of Chicago
9. University of Wisconsin-Madison
10. Indiana University
11. Princeton University
12. University of Texas

10
1. Theodore Roosevelt
2. Dwight David Eisenhower
3. Richard Nixon
4. Ronald Reagan
5. Jimmy Carter
6. George H.W. Bush
7. George W Bush
8. Barack Obama
9. Donald Trump
10. Joe Biden

BUSINESS & INDUSTRY 9♣

A	Choose a Question
2	According to an end of 2022 YouGov poll, 12 places where you buy groceries were rated favorably by half or more of millennials. Name the 12 most liked grocery stores of this generation.
3	Among the 500 companies of Forbes fortune 500, 11 US States can boast 18 or more companies on this list (2021), with 2 states having more than 50. Name the 11 states with the most Fortune 500 companies
4	According to a 2022 survey of leading hardware stores, the 16th most purchased items are plumbing supplies. Name any of the 15 most purchased items from Hardware stores (in volume, not dollar value)
5	Due to a tie at #12, 13 universities are rated in the 12 best for MBA programs by U.S. News. Name these 12 Best Business schools (or their related university)
6	According to Forbes, 9 Health insurers have over a million members as of 2022. Name any of the 11 largest insurance companies by membership.
7	In 2020, 15 companies sold more than $3.5 Billion in Beauty and Cosmetics products. L Brands is no more (Splitting into Victoria's Secret and Bath & Body Works). Name the 14 other largest companies in the Beauty field.
8	The Center for Retail Research listed 13 items that were most likely to be shoplifted in a 2019 study. Excluding the non-specific "Small Electronics" listing, Name the 12 most shoplifted items from American Retailers.
9	According to a survey by trade website textileindustry.net, Name the 13 companies that sell the most denim jeans
10	According to Car and Driver magazine, the top selling Automobiles included 3 cars, 4 SUVs and 5 pickup trucks. Name any of the 12 best selling vehicles of 2022.

Business & Industry 9♣

2
1. Aldi
2. Whole Foods
3. Trader Joe's
4. 7-Eleven
5. Kroger
6. Circle K
7. Safeway
8. Fresh Market
9. Food Lion
10. Amazon Fresh
11. Publix
12. Sprouts

3
1. New York
2. California
3. Texas
4. Illinois
5. Ohio
6. Pennsylvania
7. Virginia
8. Florida
9. Massachusetts
10. Georgia
11. Minnesota

4
1. Adhesives (Glues)
2. Work/Latex Gloves
3. Wrenches
4. Tapes
5. Keys/Door Locks
6. Light Bulbs
7. Fasteners (Screws/Nails)
8. Batteries
9. Washers (not for clothes)
10. Hinges
11. Latches
12. Handles/Door Handles
13. Wires & Ropes
14. Chains
15. Belts

5
1. Booth (University of Chicago)
2. Wharton (University of Pennsylvania)
3. Kellogg (Northwestern)
4. Stanford
5. Harvard
6. Sloan (Massachusetts Institute of Technology)
7. Yale
8. Columbia
9. Haas (California-Berkeley)
10. Ross (Michigan)
11. Tuck (Dartmouth)
12. Fuqua (Duke)
13. Stern (New York University)

6
1. Kaiser Permanente
2. Elevance Health (Anthem)
3. Health Care Service Corp (HCSC)
4. UnitedHealth Group
5. Centene
6. CVS Health (Aetna)
7. Guidewell (Florida Blue)
8. Blue Cross Blue Shield of Michigan
9. Highmark
10. Blue Cross Blue Shield of North Carolina
11. Humana

7
1. L'Oreal
2. Unilever
3. Estee Lauder
4. Proctor & Gamble
5. Coty
6. Shiseido
7. Beiersdorf
8. Johnson & Johnson
9. Amore Pacific
10. Kao
11. LVMH (Moet Hennessey Louis Vuitton)
12. Avon
13. Henkel
14. Mary Kay

8
1. Packed Meat
2. Razor Blades
3. Whiskey (Alcohol)
4. Cosmetics
5. Cheese
6. Under Arm Deodorants
7. Clothing Accessories
8. Baby Clothes
9. Jeans
10. Perfume (Cologne)
11. Athletic Wear
12. Boxed DVD/Video Games

9
1. Levi's
2. Wrangler
3. Lee
4. Diesel
5. Calvin Klein
6. Pepe Jeans London
7. True Religion
8. Armani
9. Gucci
10. Guess
11. Versace
12. Nostrum
13. Killer

10
1. Toyota Corolla
2. Toyota Highlander
3. Jeep Grand Cherokee
4. Tesla Model Y
5. Toyota Tacoma
6. Honda CR-V
7. GMC Sierra
8. Toyota Camry
9. Toyota RAV4
10. Ram Pickup
11. Chevy Silverado
12. Ford F-Serie

Colleges & Universities 10♣

A	Choose a Question

2	16 of the Top 50 Universities, according to US News, are public Institutions. Name any of these 16 public universities.

3	While the Largest Endowments go to Private schools, 13 US Public Universities currently (2023) have endowments in excess of $4 Billion. Name any of these well-funded public institutions.

4	In 1985 book about "Public Ivies," Public Colleges where you can get an Ivy League quality experience was introduced. 24 schools were spotlighted. Aside from the 8 California System schools, name any of the other 16 colleges

5	In 2023, 16 Colleges or Universities accepted 7% or less of their applicants. Name any of these 16 hardest to get into schools.

6	Seattle's University of Washington is tied with 4 other schools for the #13 spot in US News rankings of best research medical schools. Name any of the 16 best medical schools either tied or ahead of them.

7	Seton Hall in New Jersey has just under 10K students (2023) making it the 14th Largest Catholic University in the US. 13 Catholic Universities have 10,000 or more students. Name any of these 10 schools.

8	Though known predominantly for Football, The SEC was founded in 1932 with 13 Schools. Name any of the original 13 Universities of the Southeastern Conference

9	Baylor University would be at #17 on this list named the US News Top Rated Colleges West of the Mississippi River. Name any of the West's 16 Top Universities

10	Princeton, situated in Princeton, New Jersey is one of the 8 prestigious "Ivy League" schools. Name any of the 7 Other Ivy League Colleges or the 7 Cities those schools call home.

COLLEGES & UNIVERSITIES 10♣

2
1. California - Berkeley
2. California - Los Angeles (UCLA)
3. Michigan
4. Virginia
5. Florida
6. North Carolina (Chapel Hill)
7. California - Santa Barbara
8. California - Irvine
9. California - San Diego
10. Caliornia - Davis
11. Texas
12. Wisconsin - Madison
13. Illinois
14. Georgia Tech
15. Ohio State
16. Georgia

3
1. Texas
2. Texas A&M
3. California
4. Michigan
5. Virginia
6. Ohio State
7. Cal-Berkeley
8. Pittsburgh
9. Minnesota
10. North Carolina at Chapel Hill
11. Washington
12. Penn State
13. UCLA

4
1. William & Mary (VA)
2. Miami University (OH)
3. Michigan
4. North Carolina (Chapel Hill)
5. Texas
6. Vermont
7. Virginia
8. Colorado
9. Georgia Tech
10. Illinois
11. New College of Florida
12. Penn State
13. Pittsburgh
14. SUNY-Binghamton
15. Washington
16. Wisconsin

5
1. Cal-Tech
2. Harvard
3. Stanford
4. Massachusetts Institute of Technology
5. Columbia
6. Princeton
7. Curtis Institute of Music
8. Yale
9. Brown
10. Duke
11. University of Chicago
12. Dartmouth
13. Northwestern
14. Pomona College
15. Vanderbilt
16. Julliard

6
1. Harvard
2. Johns Hopkins
3. Pennsylvania (Perelman)
4. Columbia
5. Duke
6. Stanford
7. California-San Francisco
8. Vanderbilt
9. Washington University in St Louis
10. Cornell (Weill)
11. NYU (Grossman)
12. Yale
13. Mayo Clinic School of Medicine (Alix)
14. Northwestern (Feinberg)
15. Michigan
16. Pittsburgh

7
1. DePaul
2. Georgetown
3. St John's University - New York
4. Loyola - Chicago
5. Fordham
6. Boston College
7. St Louis
8. Notre Dame
9. Dayton
10. Marquette
11. Villanova
12. Loyola Marymount
13. University of San Francisco

8
1. Florida
2. Georgia
3. Kentucky
4. Tennessee
5. Vanderbilt
6. Alabama
7. Auburn
8. Louisiana State (LSU)
9. Mississippi (Ole Miss)
10. Mississippi State
11. Georgia Tech
12. Tulane
13. Sewanee (University of the South)

9
1. Stanford
2. Cal-Tech
3. Rice
4. Washington University in St. Louis
5. Cal-Berkeley
6. UCLA
7. USC
8. California -Santa Barbara
9. California - Irvine
10. California - San Diego
11. California - Davia
12. Texas
13. Pepperdine
14. Santa Clara
15. Washington
16. Texas A&M
17. Southern Methodist

10
1. Brown
2. Providence, RI
3. Columbia
4. New York, NY
5. Cornell
6. Ithaca, NY
7. Dartmouth
8. Hanover, NH
9. Harvard
10. Cambridge, MA
11. University of Pennsylvania (Penn)
12. Philadelphia, PA
13. Yale
14. New Haven, CT

COOKING J♣

A	Choose a Question

2	Aside from the Pastry Shell, Betty Crocker's Cookbook lists 11 ingredients for Chicken Pot Pie, Name them.

3	KFC uses 11 herbs and spices in their Original Recipe Fried Chicken. This recipe was reportedly found by the Chicago Tribune in a nephew of Col. Sanders scrapbook. Name these 11 Herbs and Spices

4	McCormack's keeps their Old Bay Seasoning recipe secret. Food.com offers a copycat recipe that contains 14 herbs and spices, as well as salt. Name any of these 14 Herbs and/or Spices.

5	According to the Betty Crocker Cookbook, there are 13 ingredients in their recipe for MeatLoaf, 7 of them being spices, Name them

6	A 2020 study of Google Search data revealed the 10 types of cuisines searched for more than all the others. Name them

7	With the Pasta Top 50 sellers on Amazon, there are 12 different shapes represented. Name these 12 popular pasta types.

8	Webrestaurantstore sells 15 different kinds of Kitchen knives. Name any of these 15 types of Kitchen knife.

9	According to a Mayo Clinic article, the best (healthiest) oils are those high in unsaturated (both mono- and poly-) fats. This article names 12 specific types of oils in no particular order, name these types of oils.

10	If you purchase a McCormack's two-tier chrome spice rack, it comes with 16 spices included, Name them.

COOKING J♣

2
1. Chicken
2. Peas
3. Carrots
4. Onions
5. Chicken Broth
6. Flour
7. Butter
8. Cream
9. Salt
10. Pepper
11. Thyme

3
1. Salt
2. Thyme
3. Basil
4. Oregano
5. Celery Salt
6. Black Pepper
7. Dry Mustard
8. Paprika
9. Garlic Salt
10. Ginger
11. White Pepper

4
1. Bay Leaf
2. Celery seed
3. Salt
4. Mustard
5. Black Pepper
6. Ginger
7. Paprika
8. White Pepper
9. Nutmeg
10. Cloves
11. Allspice
12. Red Pepper
13. Mace
14. Cardamom
15. Cinnamon

5
1. Ground Beef
2. Ground Pork
3. Ground Veal
4. Egg
5. Onion, Minced
6. Bread Crumbs (or Bread)
7. Worcestershire Sauce
8. Salt
9. Celery Salt
10. Pepper, Black
11. Garlic
12. Sage
13. Mustard, Dry

6
1. Chinese
2. Mexican
3. Thai
4. Indian
5. Korean
6. Japanese
7. Soul
8. Greek
9. Italian
10. Hawaiian

7
1. Spaghetti
2. Elbow macaroni
3. Linguine
4. Angel hair
5. Penne
6. Stars
7. Tortellini
8. Shells
9. Bucatini
10. Manicotti
11. Ditalini
12. Vermicelli

8
1. Chef
2. Utility
3. Cleaver
4. Paring
5. Butcher
6. Bread (Serrated)
7. Boning
8. Oyster
9. Carving
10. Cheese
11. Santoku
12. Nakiri
13. Tourne
14. Breaking
15. Cimeter (Scimitar)

9
1. Vegetable
2. Olive
3. Peanut
4. Sesame
5. Soybean
6. Avocado
7. Corn
8. Canola
9. Flaxseed
10. Pumpkin Seed
11. Walnut
12. Grapeseed

10
1. Oregano Leaves
2. Crushed Red Pepper
3. Thyme
4. Sage, Rubbed
5. Ginger, Ground
6. Garlic Salt
7. Rosemary Leaves
8. Garlic Powder
9. Cumin, Ground
10. Bay Leaves
11. Cinnamon, Ground
12. Onion Powder
13. Paprika
14. Chili Powder
15. Parsley Flake
16. Basil Leaves

DESSERTS Q♣

A	Choose a Question

2	According to the Girl Scout Website, there are 13 different kinds of cookies available for purchase for the 2023 campaign. Name these cookies.

3	There are many flavors of Jell-O brand gelatin. But only 13 with where the name is simply a fruit (ie "Lime" as opposed to "Island Pineapple") Name the 12 other fruit flavors of Jell-O according to their website

4	According to a 2022 YouGov Poll of Americans, 11 different pies were ranked as "Love it" if asked if they'd want it served on Thanksgiving. Name these 11 pies

5	Nestle got the recipe from the Toll House Inn of Massachusetts. The recipe for Toll House Cookies has 10 ingredients. Name them

6	According to the Ben & Jerry's Website, there are 12 Flavors that they currently serve that debuted in 1994 or earlier. Name any of these 12 longest running Ben & Jerry's Flavors

7	According to the online Free Dictionary, there are 17 compound words that end with -cake, like Johnnycake. Name any of the other 16

8	According to a September 2022 *Bon Appetit* article with recipe, their version of the filling for Pumpkin Pie contains 12 items. Aside from Pumpkin, name the other 11 Ingredients

9	Online Polling website Ranker.com asked what are the "most delicious kind of dessert." The Chocolate Chip Cookie is listed at #3. Name any of the 11 other sweets that filled out the top 12

10	At the end of 2022, Ben & Jerry's reported their top 10 selling flavors for the year, which were the same as they were in 2021. Name the 10 Best Selling Flavors of Ben & Jerry's Ice Cream Pints.

Desserts Q♣

2
1. Raspberry Rally
2. Adventurefuls
3. Caramel Chocolate Chip
4. Caramel DeLites/Samoas
5. Do-Si-dos/Peanut Butter Sandwich
6. Girl Scout S'mores
7. Lemonades
8. Lemon-Ups
9. Tagalongs/Peanut Butter Patties
10. Thin Mints
11. Toast-Yay!
12. Toffee-tastic
13. Trefoils

3
1. Mango
2. Orange
3. Peach
4. Strawberry
5. Apricot
6. Watermelon
7. Cherry
8. Raspberry
9. Cranberry
10. Lemon
11. Strawberry
12. Grape

4
1. Apple
2. Pumpkin
3. Chocolate
4. Cherry
5. Banana Cream
6. Pecan
7. Peach
8. Lemon Meringue
9. Blueberry
10. Boston Creme
11. Coconut Cream

5
1. All Purpose Flour
2. Semi-Sweet Chocolate Morsels
3. Chopped Nuts
4. Butter
5. Eggs
6. Granulated Sugar (White)
7. Brown Sugar
8. Vanilla Extract
9. Baking Soda
10. Salt

6
1. Cherry Garcia
2. New York Super Fudge Chunk
3. Chocolate Chip Cookie Dough
4. Chocolate Fudge Brownie
5. Vanilla Caramel Fudge
6. Coffee Toffee Bar Crunch
7. Coffee, Coffee, BuzzBuzzBuzz
8. Mint Chocolate Cookie
9. Chunky Monkey
10. Chubby Hubby
11. Pistachio Pistachio
12. Peanut Butter Cup

7
1. Pancake
2. Ashcake
3. Hoecake
4. Cupcake
5. hotcake
6. Teacake
7. oatcake
8. seedcake
9. millcake
10. beefcake
11. corncake
12. shortcake
13. fruitcake
14. poundcake
15. friedcake
16. cheesecake

8
1. Sugar
2. Salt
3. Eggs
4. Condensed Milk
5. Heavy Cream
6. Ginger
7. Cinnamon
8. Cloves
9. Nutmeg
10. Maple Syrup
11. Vanilla Extract

9
1. Ice Cream
2. Brownies
3. Chocolate
4. Milkshake
5. Cheesecake
6. Cake
7. Doughnut
8. Cookies
9. Sundaes
10. Cinnamon Roll
11. Pies

10
1. Half-Baked
2. Cherry Garcia
3. Chocolate Chip Cookie Dough
4. Chocolate Fudge Brownie
5. Tonight Dough
6. Strawberry Cheesecake
7. Phish Food
8. Americone Dream
9. Chunky Monkey
10. Brownie Batter Core

DINING K♣

A	Choose a Question

2	Celebritynetworth.com lists 14 Chefs or Restaurateurs who have a net worth of greater than $50 million. Name any of the 14 wealthiest people of the culinary world

3	China, which includes Hong Kong and Macao, has 14 Michelin 3 star restaurants. Only 16 other countries can boast even one. Name them.

4	A 12 Course meal normally has one course repeated, leaving 11 courses in a typical dinner of this type. Name them

5	According to Grubhub, 14 of the 50 most ordered foods of 2022 were from Asian Cuisines (ie. Indian, Chinese, etc.). Name any of these 14 most popular Asian food items for home delivery

6	If you were to build your own Pizza, from World Famous Frank Pepe's in New Haven, CT, you would have the choice of 11 toppings, aside from Meat, Cheese, and Sauce. Name them.

7	The 50 most profitable (in terms of Gross Sales) independent restaurants in the USA are located within 13 cities' Metro Areas. Name the cities that are home to America's busiest restaurants.

8	Emily Post's website published an article of the "10 Must Know Table Manners." Name them.

9	Online Public Polling site Ranker.com lists "The Most Delicious Types of Sushi." Name any of the types of sushi rolls in the Top 12

10	According to Emily Post, a properly set Formal Table setting has 18 pieces, 11 of which are utensils. Name them

DINING K♣

2
1. Kimbal Musk
2. Gordon Ramsay
3. Jamie Oliver
4. Nobu Matsuhisaa
5. Wolfgang Puck
6. Rachael Ray
7. Emeril Lagasse
8. Guy Fieri
9. Bobby Flay
10. Ina Garten
11. Jose Andres
12. Ree Drummond
13. Thomas Keller
14. Vikram Vij

3
1. France
2. Japan
3. USA
4. Spain
5. Italy
6. Germany
7. United Kingdom
8. Switzerland
9. Singapore
10. Belgium
11. Denmark
12. Netherlands
13. South Korea
14. Austria
15. Sweden
16. Taiwan

4
1. Hors d'oeuvre
2. Amuse-Bouche
3. Soup
4. Appetizer
5. Salad
6. Fish
7. First Main Course
8. Palate cleanser
9. Second Main course
10. Cheese
11. Dessert
12. Mignardise

5
1. Miso Soup
2. California Roll
3. Chicken Tikka Masala
4. Spicy Tuna Roll
5. Gyoza
6. Shrimp Tempura Roll
7. Crab Rangoon
8. White Rice
9. Thai Iced Tea
10. Salmon Avocado Roll
11. Wonton Soup
12. Hummus
13. Seaweed Salad
14. Sesame Chicken

6
1. Onions
2. Mushrooms
3. Garlic, Fresh
4. Green Peppers
5. Red Peppers (Roasted)
6. Spinach
7. Cherry Peppers (Hot)
8. Broccoli
9. Basil, Fresh
10. Olives (Imported Abruzo)
11. Oregano

7
1. Las Vegas NV
2. Miami, FL
3. New York, NY
4. Washington, DC
5. Orlando, FL
6. Chicago, IL
7. Los Angeles, CA
8. Indianapolis IN)
9. Raleigh NC
10. Nashville, TN
11. Boston MA
12. Philadelphia, PA
13. Houston TX

8
1. Chew with your mouth closed
2. Put away and silence your Smartphone
3. Hold & Use Utensils Correctly
4. Wash before dinner
5. Use your Napkin
6. Finish Chewing before Drinking
7. Pace yourself with others
8. No Slouching, No Elbows on Table while eating
9. Don't reach across table (ask for items to be passed)
10. Take part in conversation

9
1. Tiger (shrimp Tempura)
2. California
3. Dragon
4. Spicy Tuna
5. Rainbow
6. Spider
7. Spicy Salmon
8. Shrimp Killer
9. Philadelphia
10. Dynamite
11. Hot Night
12. Alaskan

10
1. Butter Knife
2. Dessert Fork
3. Dessert Spoon
4. Fish Fork
5. Entree Fork
6. Salad Fork
7. Salad Knife
8. Entree Knife
9. Fish Knife
10. Soup Spoon
11. Oyster Fork

ELEMENTARY A♦

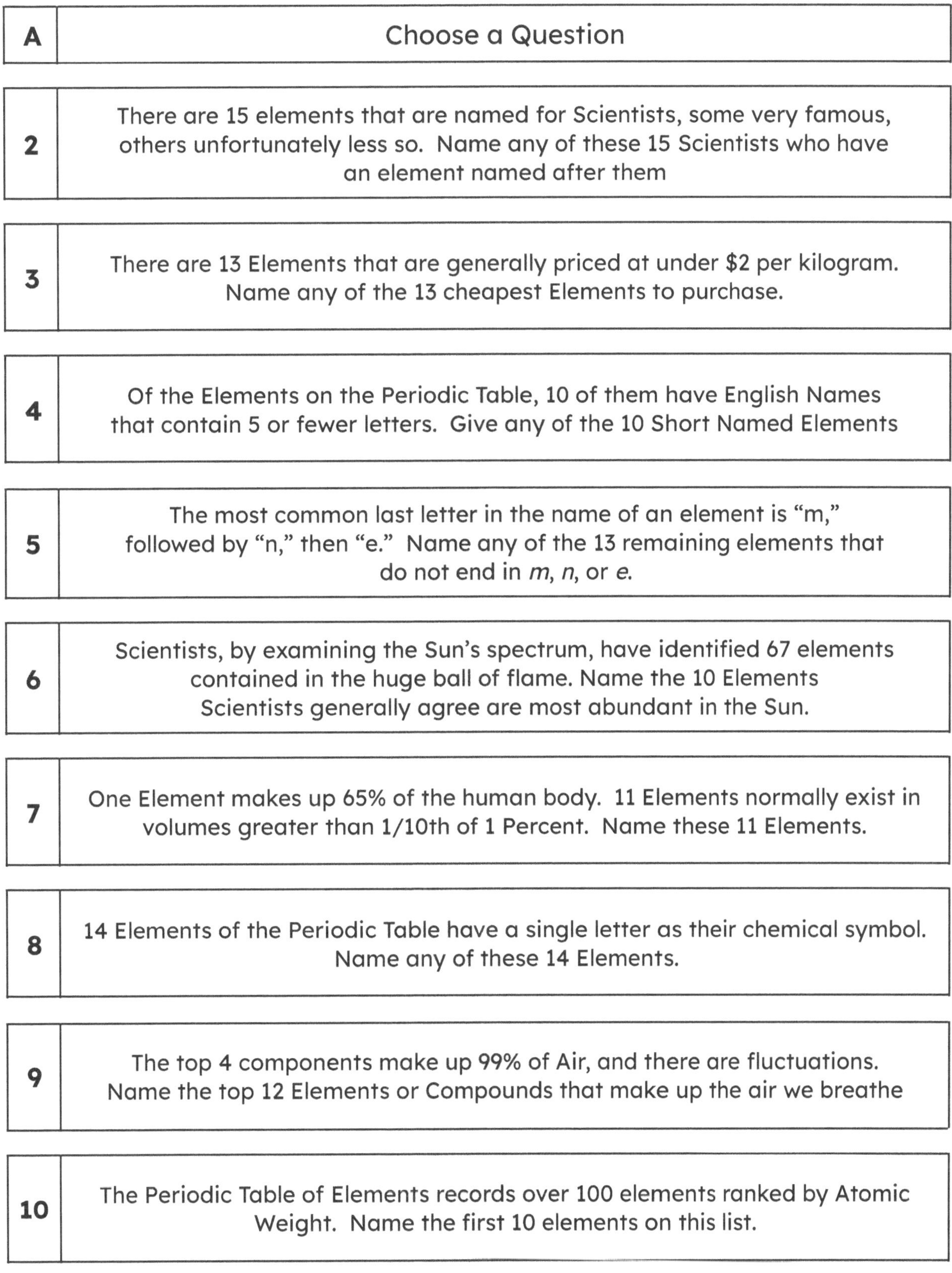

A	Choose a Question
2	There are 15 elements that are named for Scientists, some very famous, others unfortunately less so. Name any of these 15 Scientists who have an element named after them
3	There are 13 Elements that are generally priced at under $2 per kilogram. Name any of the 13 cheapest Elements to purchase.
4	Of the Elements on the Periodic Table, 10 of them have English Names that contain 5 or fewer letters. Give any of the 10 Short Named Elements
5	The most common last letter in the name of an element is "m," followed by "n," then "e." Name any of the 13 remaining elements that do not end in *m*, *n*, or *e*.
6	Scientists, by examining the Sun's spectrum, have identified 67 elements contained in the huge ball of flame. Name the 10 Elements Scientists generally agree are most abundant in the Sun.
7	One Element makes up 65% of the human body. 11 Elements normally exist in volumes greater than 1/10th of 1 Percent. Name these 11 Elements.
8	14 Elements of the Periodic Table have a single letter as their chemical symbol. Name any of these 14 Elements.
9	The top 4 components make up 99% of Air, and there are fluctuations. Name the top 12 Elements or Compounds that make up the air we breathe
10	The Periodic Table of Elements records over 100 elements ranked by Atomic Weight. Name the first 10 elements on this list.

Elementary A♦

2
1. Marie Curie
2. Johan Gadolin
3. Albert Einstein
4. Enrico Fermi
5. Dmitri Mendeleev
6. Alfred Nobel
7. Ernest Lawrence
8. Ernest Rutherford
9. Glenn Seaborg
10. Niels Bohr
11. Lise Meitner
12. Wilhelm Roentgen
13. Nicolaus Copernicus
14. Georgy Flyorov
15. Yuri Oganessian

3
1. Chlorine
2. Sulfur
3. Carbon
4. Nitrogen
5. Oxygen
6. Barium
7. Iron
8. Argon
9. Arsenic
10. Hydrogen
11. Silicon
12. Aluminum
13. Manganese

4
1. Boron
2. Neon
3. Argon
4. Iron
5. Zinc
6. Tin
7. Xenon
8. Gold
9. Lead
10. Radon

5
1. Phosphorus
2. Sulfur
3. Cobalt
4. Nickel
5. Copper
6. Zinc
7. Arsenic
8. Silver
9. Antimony
10. Gold
11. Mercury
12. Lead
13. Bismuth

6
1. Hydrogen
2. Helium
3. Oxygen
4. Carbon
5. Nitrogen
6. Silicon
7. Magnesium
8. Neon
9. Iron
10. Sulfur

7
1. Oxygen
2. Carbon
3. Hydrogen
4. Nitrogen
5. Calcium
6. Phosphorus
7. Sulfur
8. Sodium
9. Chlorine
10. Magnesium

8
1. Hydrogen
2. Boron
3. Carbon
4. Nitrogen
5. Oxygen
6. Fluorine
7. Phosphorus
8. Sulfur
9. Potassium (K)
10. Vanadium
11. Yttrium
12. Iodine
13. Tungsten (W)
14. Uranium

9
1. Nitrogen
2. Oxygen
3. Water (Vapor)
4. Argon
5. Carbon Dioxide
6. Neon
7. Methane
8. Helium
9. Krypton
10. Hydrogen
11. Xenon
12. Ozone

10
1. Hydrogen
2. Helium
3. Lithium
4. Beryllium
5. Boron
6. Carbon
7. Nitrogen
8. Oxygen
9. Fluorine
10. Neon

EUROPE 2♦

A	Choose a Question
2	The Danube River flows nearly 1800 miles into the Black Sea. It passes 4 National Capitals and through or borders 10 Countries. Name these 10 countries.
3	The Soviet Union, during the Cold War, began either annexing or controlling most of Eastern Europe. Name the 10 other current countries that made up the "Iron Curtain" besides Russia
4	The 15 Northernmost National Capitals fall within the boundaries of Europe. Dublin, Ireland is 11th on this list. Name the 10 Northernmost Capitals of the World.
5	19 European Countries use the Euro abandoning their own historical currency. With duplications 13 former names for currencies have been retired. Name these 13 historical European currencies.
6	12 European Countries still hold on to some form of Royalty in their Government. Name these 12 European Nations.
7	The Mediterranean Sea borders 21 countries, 11 of them on the Mainland of Europe with 2 European Islands. Name these 13 European Nations.
8	14 European Countries have flags made of simply 3 equal tri-colored stripes and nothing more. 5 are Vertical, 9 are Horizontal. Name these 14 countries.
9	Half of the world's 10 smallest countries lie within the continent of Europe. Name the 10 smallest (in terms of Area) countries of the World
10	12 Metro Areas in Europe have over 4 million in population. Rome, Italy just misses this list at #13. Name the 12 most populous cities or areas in Europe.

EUROPE 2♦

2
1. Germany
2. Austria
3. Hungary
4. Slovakia
5. Croatia
6. Serbia
7. Romania
8. Bulgaria
9. Moldova
10. Ukraine

3
1. Poland
2. Finland
3. Romania
4. Czechia (Czechoslovakia)
5. Slovakia (Czechoslovakia)
6. Germany
7. Bulgaria
8. Poland
9. Hungary
10. Albania

4
1. Reykjavik, Iceland
2. Helsinki, Finland
3. Oslo, Norway
4. Tallinn, Estonia
5. Stockholm, Sweden
6. Riga, Latvia
7. Moscow, Russia
8. Copenhagen, Denmark
9. Vilnius, Lithuania
10. Minsk, Belarus

5
1. Mark
2. Schilling
3. Franc
4. Pound
5. Lira
6. Kroon
7. Markka
8. Drachma
9. Guilder
10. Escudo
11. Koruna
12. Tolar
13. Peseta

6
1. Andorra
2. Belgium
3. Denmark
4. Liechtenstein
5. Luxembourg
6. Monaco
7. The Netherlands
8. Norway
9. Spain
10. Sweden
11. The Vatican
12. UK

7
1. Albania
2. Bosnia and Herzegovina
3. Croatia
4. France
5. Greece
6. Italy
7. Monaco
8. Montenegro
9. Slovenia
10. Spain
11. Turkey
12. Malta
13. Cyprus

8
1. Belgium
2. France
3. Ireland
4. Italy
5. Romania
6. Austria
7. Bulgaria
8. Estonia
9. Germany
10. Hungary
11. Lithuania
12. Luxembourg
13. Netherlands
14. Russia

9
1. Vatican City (The Holy See)
2. Monaco
3. Nauru
4. Tuvalu
5. San Marino
6. Liechtenstein
7. Marshall Islands
8. St. Kitts and Nevis
9. Maldives
10. Malta

10
1. Moscow, Russia
2. Istanbul, Turkey
3. London, England
4. Paris, France
5. Madrid, Spain
6. Milan, Italy
7. Ruhr Valley, Germany (18 cities, most notably Dortmund)
8. St Petersburg, Russia
9. Barcelona, Spain
10. Rhein Sud (Cologne-Bonn), Germany
11. Berlin, Germany
12. Naples, Italy

FAMOUS ACTORS 3♦

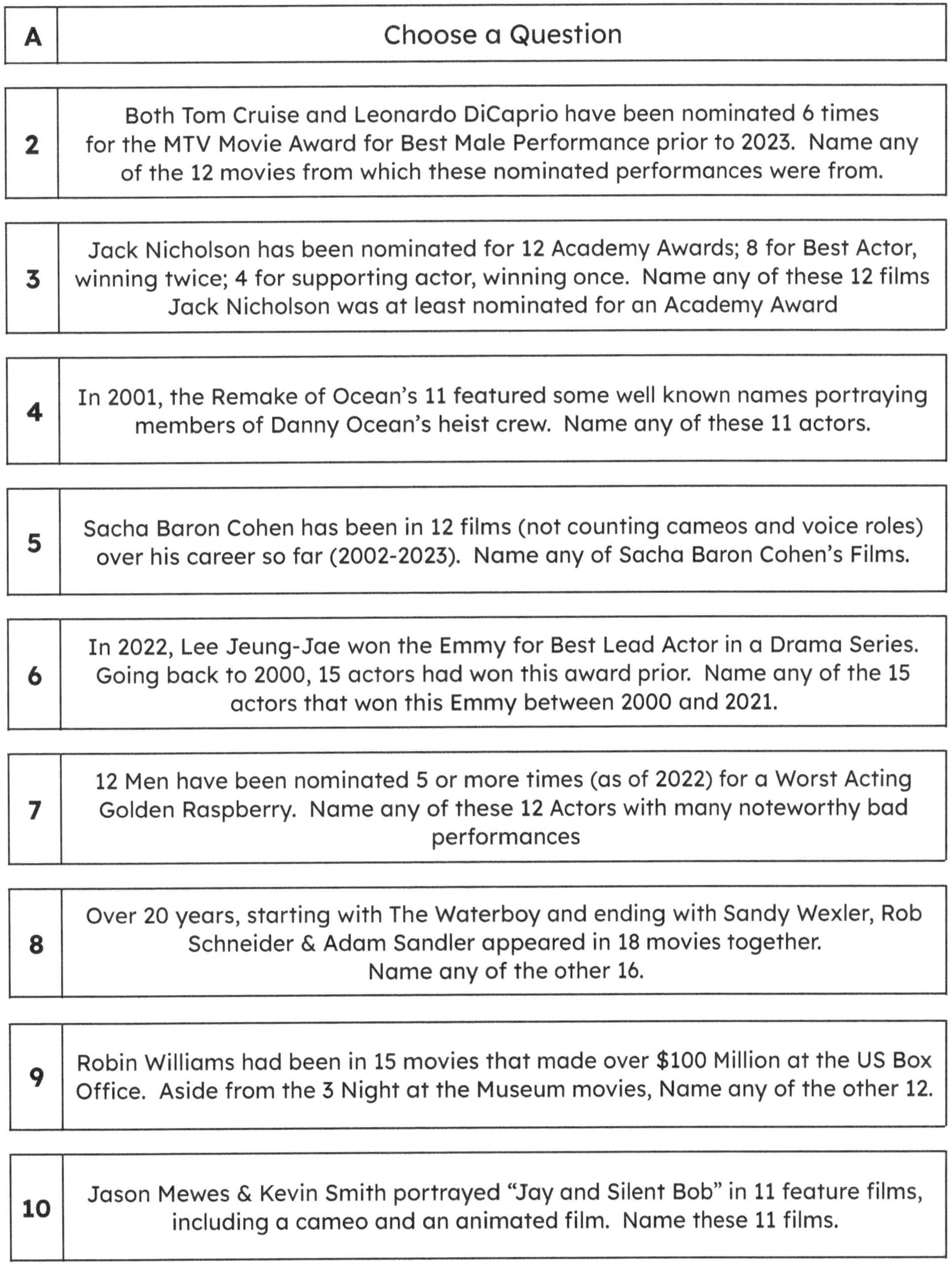

A	Choose a Question
2	Both Tom Cruise and Leonardo DiCaprio have been nominated 6 times for the MTV Movie Award for Best Male Performance prior to 2023. Name any of the 12 movies from which these nominated performances were from.
3	Jack Nicholson has been nominated for 12 Academy Awards; 8 for Best Actor, winning twice; 4 for supporting actor, winning once. Name any of these 12 films Jack Nicholson was at least nominated for an Academy Award
4	In 2001, the Remake of Ocean's 11 featured some well known names portraying members of Danny Ocean's heist crew. Name any of these 11 actors.
5	Sacha Baron Cohen has been in 12 films (not counting cameos and voice roles) over his career so far (2002-2023). Name any of Sacha Baron Cohen's Films.
6	In 2022, Lee Jeung-Jae won the Emmy for Best Lead Actor in a Drama Series. Going back to 2000, 15 actors had won this award prior. Name any of the 15 actors that won this Emmy between 2000 and 2021.
7	12 Men have been nominated 5 or more times (as of 2022) for a Worst Acting Golden Raspberry. Name any of these 12 Actors with many noteworthy bad performances
8	Over 20 years, starting with The Waterboy and ending with Sandy Wexler, Rob Schneider & Adam Sandler appeared in 18 movies together. Name any of the other 16.
9	Robin Williams had been in 15 movies that made over $100 Million at the US Box Office. Aside from the 3 Night at the Museum movies, Name any of the other 12.
10	Jason Mewes & Kevin Smith portrayed "Jay and Silent Bob" in 11 feature films, including a cameo and an animated film. Name these 11 films.

FAMOUS ACTORS 3♦

2
1. A Few Good Men
2. The Firm
3. Jerry Maguire
4. Mission Impossible 2
5. The Last Samurai
6. Top Gun: Maverick
7. Romeo & Juliet
8. Titanic
9. Catch Me If You Can
10. The Aviator
11. The Wolf of Wall Street
12. The Revenant

3
1. One Flew over the Cuckoo's Nest
2. As Good as it Gets
3. Terms of Endearment
4. FIve Easy Pieces
5. The Last Detail
6. Chinatown
7. Prizzi's Honor
8. Ironweed
9. About Schmidt
10. Easy Rider
11. Reds
12. A Few Good Men

4
1. George Clooney
2. Bernie Mac
3. Brad Pitt
4. Elliot Gould
5. Casey Affleck
6. Scott Caan
7. Eddie Jemison
8. Don Cheadle
9. Qin Shaobo
10. Carl Reiner
11. Matt Damon

5
1. Borat Subsequent Moviefilm
2. The Trial Of the Chicago 7
3. Alice Through the Looking Glass
4. Grimsby
5. Les Miserables
6. The Dictator
7. Hugo
8. Bruno
9. Sweeney Todd: The Demon Barber of Fleet Street
10. Borat! Cultural Learnings of America for Make Benefit Glorious Nation of Kazakhstan
11. Talladega Nights: The Ballad of Ricky Bobby
12. Ali G Indahouse

6
1. Josh O'Connor
2. Jeremy Strong
3. Billy Porter
4. Matthew Rhys
5. Sterling K Brown
6. Rami Malek
7. Jon Hamm
8. Bryan Cranston
9. Jeff Daniels
10. Damien Lewis
11. Kyle Chandler
12. James Spader
13. Kiefer Sutherland
14. James Gandolfini
15. Michael Chiklis

7
1. Sylvester Stallone
2. Adam Sandler
3. Kevin Costner
4. John Travolta
5. Nicolas Cage
6. Eddie Murphy
7. Arnold Schwarzenegger
8. Burt Reynolds
9. Ben Affleck
10. Johnny Depp
11. Bruce WIllis
12. Tyler Perry

8
1. Big Daddy
2. Deuce Bigalow: Male Gigolo
3. Little Nicky
4. The Animal
5. Mr.Deeds
6. The Hot Chick
7. Eight Crazy Nights
8. 50 First Dates
9. The Longest Yard
10. Click
11. I Now Pronounce you Chuck and Larry
12. You Don't Mess with the Zohan
13. Bed Time Stories
14. Grown Ups
15. Jack and Jill
16. The Ridiculous Six

9
1. Jumanji : Welcome to the Jungle
2. Mrs. Doubtfire
3. Aladdin
4. Happy Feet
5. Good Will Hunting
6. Patch Adams
7. Robots
8. The Birdcage
9. Good Morning Vietnam
10. Hook
11. Lee Daniels' The Butler
12. Jumanji

10
1. Clerks 3
2. Jay and Silent Bob Reboot
3. Jay and Silent Bob's Super Groovy Cartoon Movie
4. Clerks 2
5. Jay and Silent Bob Strike Back
6. Scream 3
7. Dogma
8. Chasing Amy
9. Mallrats
10. Clerks
11. Madness to the Method

FAMOUS ACTRESSES 4♦

A	Choose a Question
2	Meryl Streep has been nominated for 17 Best Leading Actress Oscars, winning twice for *Sophie's Choice* and *The Iron Lady*. Name any of the other 15 films in which she was nominated for Best Actress
3	In the 50 years since 1973, 13 Actresses have won the Emmy Award for Best Actress in a Drama Series 2 or more times. Name any of these 13 multi-honored women.
4	Six women portrayed "Angels" in the original Charlie's Angels (1976-81) Television series. Another 4 Angels were named in the original Movie Reboots (2000, 2003). Name any of the 10 Actresses who portrayed these detectives.
5	In 2003-4 & 2012-15, the Kids' Choice awards had an award for "Favorite Female Buttkicker." 4 Actresses won the award, and another 12 were nominated. Name any of these 16 action-based nominated Actresses from TV or Film.
6	According to a YouGov Poll (Q2, 2023), 18 Actresses were liked by 70% or more of Respondents. Name any of these 18 most popular Actresses.
7	Zendaya won the Emmy for Best Leading Actress in a Drama in 2022 (& 2020) making her the 16th woman to win this award since 2001. Name any of the other 15 award winning Actresses.
8	In 2006 Helen Mirren won the Academy Award for Best Actress for portraying Queen Elizabeth. In the 15 years after (2007-22) 15 different women won this award. Name these 15 Academy Award winning Actresses.
9	The "Most Popular Show in the World," Baywatch featured 15 actresses portraying Lifeguards (through its first 8 seasons, before spinoffs). Name any of these 15 Actresses.
10	In 2018, Ocean's Eight was released, retelling the story with a mostly Female cast. Name any of the 12 actresses whose names appear before the scrolling end credits of this film.

Famous Actresses 4♦

2
1. The French Lieutenant's Woman
2. Silkwood
3. Out of Africa
4. Ironweed
5. A Cry in the Dark
6. Postcards from the Edge
7. The Bridges of Madison County
8. One True Thing
9. Music of the Heart
10. The Devil Wears Prada
11. Doubt
12. Julie & Julia
13. August: Osage County
14. Florence Foster Jenkins
15. The Post

3
1. Zendaya
2. Claire Danes
3. Juliana Marguiles
4. Glenn Close
5. Allison Janney
6. Edie Falco
7. Kathy Baker
8. Sela Ward
9. Patricia Wettig
10. Dana Delaney
11. Tyne Daly
12. Sharon Gless
13. Michael Learned

4
1. Farrah Fawcett
2. Kate Jackson
3. Jaclyn Smith
4. Cheryl Ladd
5. Shelley Hack
6. Tanya Roberts
7. Cameron Diaz
8. Drew Barrymore
9. Lucy Liu
10. Demi Moore

5
1. Sarah Michelle Gellar
2. Jennifer Love Hewitt
3. Kristen Stewart
4. Jennifer Lawrence
5. Angelina Jolie
6. Jessica Alba
7. Zhang Zhi
8. Halle Berry
9. Beyonce
10. Anne Hathaway
11. Scarlett Johansson
12. Sandra Bullock
13. Jena Malone
14. Evangeline Lilly
15. Zoe Saldana
16. Eliot Page

6
1. Betty White
2. Audrey Hepburn
3. Lucille Ball
4. Sandra Bullock
5. Julia Roberts
6. Goldie Hawn
7. Carol Burnett
8. Jamie Lee Curtis
9. Judy Garland
10. Olivia Newton John
11. Anne Hathaway
12. Marilyn Monroe
13. Sally Field
14. Mary Tyler Moore
15. Shirley Temple
16. Meryl Streep
17. Halle Berry
18. Reese Witherspoon

7
1. Olivia Colman
2. Jodie Comer
3. Claire Foy
4. Elisabeth Moss
5. Tatiana Maslany
6. Viola Davis
7. Julianna Marguiles
8. Claire Danes
9. Kyra Sedgwick
10. Glenn Close
11. Sally Field
12. Mariska Hargitay
13. Patricia Arquetta
14. Allison Janney
15. Edie Falco

8
1. Michelle Yeoh
2. Jessica Chastain
3. Frances McDormand
4. Renee Zellweger
5. Olivia Colman
6. Emma Stone
7. Brie Larson
8. Julianne Moore
9. Cate Blanchett
10. Jennifer Lawrence
11. Meryl Streep
12. Natalie Portman
13. Sandra Bullock
14. Kate Winslet
15. Marion Cotillard

9
1. Shawn Weatherly
2. Erika Eleniak
3. Nicole Eggert
4. Pamela Anderson
5. Alexandra Paul
6. Yasmine Bleeth
7. Heather Campbell
8. Gena Lee Nolin
9. Donna D'Errico
10. Traci Bingham
11. Nancy Valen
12. Carmen Electra
13. Kelly Packard
14. Angelica Bridges
15. Marliece Andrada

10
1. Sandra Bullock
2. Cate Blanchett
3. Anne Hatthaway
4. Mindy Kaling
5. Sarah Paulson
6. Awkwafina
7. Rihanna
8. Helena Bonham Carter
9. Elisabeth Ashley
10. Dana Ivey
11. Marlo Thomas
12. Mary louise Wilson

FILMS 5♦

A	Choose a Question

2	As of the end of 2022, and adjusting for inflation, 10 movies had worldwide gross box office receipts of $2.5 Trillion or more (in 2022 dollars). Name any of these 10 films that dominated theaters in their time.

3	According to BoxOfficeMojo, As of 2022, 15 documentaries have a lifetime gross in excess of $20 Million. Name any of these 15 documentaries.

4	The Positions of #1, #3, #7, & #10 on the list of top-grossing "G" rated films of all time are occupied by the Toy Story Franchise. Name any other of these top 20 grossing family friendly films

5	In 2015, the Writers Guild of America put out a list of the 101 funniest screenplays of all time. Bridesmaids (2011) appeared at #16. Name any of the 15 funniest movies according to screenwriters

6	Online Polling Website Ranker.Com asked its visitors to rank the Best Romantic-Comedy movies of all time. Name any of the films that came in the Top 15.

7	Hollywood, the US Film Industry, is number 1 in Films made by some margin. Based on theatrical release, 12 other countries Film industries have released 1,000 or more films. Name these 12 countries.

8	Only 17 Sports Movies have made over $100 Million at the Box Office. 4 of these are "Rocky" movies. Name any of the other 13 most money-making Sports Films

9	Christmas Favorite, "Love Actually" has a star-studded cast. Name any of the 17 Actors or Actresses that have their name in the Opening Credits

10	Though there are many, many subgenres of horror film, the LA Film School lists 10 genres in their study guide deemed popular and important. Name any of these 10 subgenres of Horror movies.

FILMS 5♦

2
1. Gone with the Wind
2. Avatar
3. Titanic
4. Star Wars
5. Avengers: Endgame
6. The Sound of Music
7. E.T. The Extra-Terrestrial
8. The Ten Commandments
9. Doctor Zhivago
10. Star Wars: the Force Awakens.

3
1. Fahrenheit 9/11
2. March of the Penguins
3. Justin Bieber: Never say Never
4. This is It (Michael Jackson Doc)
5. Under the Sea 3D
6. 2016: Obama's America
7. Earth
8. Chimpanzee
9. One Direction: This is Us
10. Born to Be Wild
11. Part of Me (Katy Perry Doc)
12. Sicko
13. An Inconvenient Truth
14. Won't you be my Neighbor
15. Bowling for Columbine

4
1. The Lion King
2. Finding Nemo
3. Monsters, Inc
4. Monsters University
5. Cars
6. Wall-E
7. Beauty and the Beast
8. Aladdin
9. Ratatouille
10. Gone With the Wind
11. Cars 2
12. The Polar Express
13. Snow White and the Seven Dwarfs
14. Tarzan
15. A Bug's Life
16. The Sound of Music

5
1. Annie Hall
2. Some Like it Hot
3. Groundhog Day
4. Airplane
5. Tootsie
6. Young Frankenstein
7. Dr Strangelove (or How I Learned to Stop Worrying and Love the Bomb
8. Blazing Saddles
9. Monty Python and the Holy Grail
10. National Lampoon's Animal House
11. This is Spinal Tap
12. The Producers
13. The Big Lebowski
14. Ghostbusters
15. When Harry Met Sally

6
1. 10 Things I Hate About you
2. The Proposal
3. While You Were Sleeping
4. You've Got Mail
5. The Princess Bride
6. Sweet Home Alabama
7. Clueless
8. How to Lose a Guy in 10 Days
9. Pretty Woman
10. The Princess Diaries
11. 50 First Dates
12. Legally Blonde
13. Overboard
14. Sleepless in Seattle
15. When Harry Met Sally

7
1. United Kingdom
2. France
3. China
4. Bollywood (India)
5. Germany
6. Canada
7. South Korea
8. Italy
9. Japan
10. Spain
11. Russia
12. Turkey

8
1. The Blind Side
2. The Water Boy
3. The Longest Yard
4. Jerry Maguire
5. Talladega Nights: the Ballad of Ricky Bobby
6. Sea Biscuit
7. Blades of Glory
8. Ford v. Ferrari
9. Remember the Titans
10. The Karate Kid Part II
11. Dodgeball: A True Underdog Story
12. A League of Their Own
13. Million Dollar Baby

9
1. Colin Firth
2. Emma Thompson
3. Hugh Grant
4. Laura Linney
5. Liam Neeson
6. Martine McCutcheon
7. Andrew Lincoln
8. Chiwetel Ejiofor
9. Gregor Fisher
10. Heike Makatsch
11. Keira Knightley
12. Kris Marshall
13. Lucia Moniz
14. Martin Freeman
15. Rodrigo Santoro
16. Thomas Sangster
17. Rowan Atkinson

10
1. Demonic
2. Paranormal
3. Monster
4. Slasher
5. Zombie
6. Gore (Splatter)
7. Witchcraft
8. Vampire
9. Psychological
10. Comedic

FINANCE & COMMERCE 6♦

A	Choose a Question

2	The 2009 Troubled Assets Relief Program gave out $200 Billion to Banks and Financial Institutions. 17 of these received between $3 and $25 Billion dollars. Name any of these 17 Financial Institutions.

3	FINRA, the securities regulator, details 10 reported economic indicators every investor should know. Name any of these 10 regular economic reports.

4	If you were to alphabetize the Dow Jones Industrial Average 30 stocks by Ticker Symbol, Honeywell (HON) would be 13th on the list. Name any of the 12 companies whose symbol would be alphabetically before HON

5	Because of political infighting over debt repayment, the USA was downgraded to AA+ by Standard and Poors in 2011, leaving 11 countries with better credit than the USA. Name these 11 AAA rated countries.

6	Understanding they are very volatile and this list can change by the second. Name the 10 most valuable Cryptocurrencies, by total value (Market Capitalization) As of February 1, 2023

7	There are 18 Stock Exchanges in 12 countries that have a market capitalization Greater than $1.5 Trillion. Leaving out Euronext, which is spread between 7 European nations, name the 12 Countries with the largest stock exchanges

8	The United States is 53rd on the list of countries ranked by tax rate from High to low. There are 18 countries with effective tax rates at 36% or higher. Name these 18 countries with the highest tax rates.

9	According to a publication of a leading fraud prevention firm, there are 10 kinds of fraud that are most common and for which we must be on watch. Name these 10 common financial deceptions

10	10 of the 11 the largest publicly traded companies are listed on American Exchanges. Name the 11 largest companies in the World in value (FEB 2020))

FINANCE & COMMERCE 6♦

2
1. Wells Fargo
2. JP Morgan Chase
3. Citigroup
4. Bank of America
5. Morgan Stanley
6. Goldman Sachs
7. Bank of America
8. PNC Financial
9. US Bancorp
10. Capital One
11. Regions
12. SunTrust
13. FIfth Third Bank
14. Hartford Financial
15. American Express
16. BB&T
17. Bank of New York/Mellon

3
1. GDP
2. Non farm Payrolls
3. Unemployment
4. Consumer Price Index
5. Producer Price Index
6. Consumer Confidence Index
7. Consumer Sentiment Index
8. Retail Sales
9. Durable Goods Orders
10. Federal Reserve Interest Rate

4
1. Apple (AAPL)
2. Amgen (AMGN)
3. American Express (AXP)
4. Boeing (BA)
5. Caterpillar Tractor (CAT)
6. Salesforce (CRM)
7. Cisco (CSCO)
8. Chevron (CVX)
9. Disney (DIS)
10. Dow (DOW)
11. Goldman Sachs (GS)
12. Home Depot (HD)

5
1. Australia
2. Canada
3. Denmark
4. Germany
5. Liechtenstein
6. Luxembourg
7. Netherlands
8. Norway
9. Singapore
10. Sweden
11. Switzerland

6
1. Bitcoin
2. Ethereum
3. Tether
4. USD Coin
5. Binance Coin
6. Ripple
7. Cardano
8. Binance USD
9. Solana
10. Polkadot

7
1. USA
2. China
3. Japan
4. Hong Kong
5. India
6. United Kingdom
7. Canada
8. Saudi Arabia
9. Switzerland
10. Germany
11. Australia
12. South Korea

8
1. Denmark
2. France
3. Belgium
4. Sweden
5. Italy
6. Austria
7. Finland
8. Cuba
9. Norway
10. Netherlands
11. Luxembourg
12. Germany
13. Greece
14. Montenegro
15. Slovenia
16. Federated States of Micronesia
17. Algeria
18. Iceland

9
1. Identity Theft (Loan/Credit Fraud)
2. Advance Fee Fraud
3. Fake Check Fraud
4. Tax Refund Fraud
5. Fraudulent Charities
6. Credit Card Fraud
7. Financial Account Takeovers
8. Ponzi Schemes (Investment Fraud)
9. Small Business Fraud (Embezzlement, Funds Misuse)
10. Romance Scams

10
1. Apple
2. Microsoft
3. Aramco
4. Alphabet
5. Amazon
6. Berkshire Hathaway
7. Tesla
8. NVIDIA
9. UnitedHeath Group
10. Visa
11. Exxon Mobil

First Wordplay 7♦

A	Choose a Question

2	Thesaurus.com lists 12 synonyms for criminal. Name any of these 12 words.

3	According to Thesaurus.com, there are 15 close synonyms to the word "storm," referring to a weather event. Name those 15 words

4	Dictionary.com lists 12 compound words that begin with the prefix, "Break-," which are between 7 and 14 letters long. Name any of these 12 words.

5	There are 18 9-letter compound words listed at the Free Dictionary that begin with "Fire." Name any of these 18 words.

6	Dictionary.com lists 18 compound words that begin with the prefix hair-, that are 9 letters in length or shorter. Name any of these 18 "hair" words

7	According to freedictionary.com, there are 18 five-letter words that when combined with the ending -ball create a valid compound word. Name any of these 18 words

8	We asked an AI Chatbot to name the first 15 adjectives that come to its mind when it thinks of "Evil." Name any of these 15 words.

9	There are 14 words that end with the double Z, that are between 3 and 10 letters in length, inclusive. Name any of these 14 words

10	There are 14 compound words on the Free Dictionary end with -wash, and are either 7, 8, or 9 letters long. Name any of these 14 words

First Wordplay 7♦

2
1. Convict
2. Crook
3. Culprit
4. Felon
5. Fugitive
6. Gangster
7. Hoodlum
8. Hooligan
9. Lawbreaker
10. Mobster
11. Offender
12. Thug

3
1. Blizzard
2. Cloudburst
3. Cyclone
4. Disturbance
5. Downpour
6. Gale
7. Gust
8. Hurricane
9. Monsoon
10. Precipitation
11. Snowstorm
12. Squall
13. Tempest
14. Tornado
15. Twister

4
1. Breakup
2. Breakage
3. breakout
4. breakable
5. breakaway
6. breakneck
7. breakdown
8. breakeven
9. breakfast
10. breakfront
11. breakwater
12. breakthrough

5
1. Fireplace
2. Firestone
3. Firelight
4. Firebreak
5. Firethorn
6. Fireboard
7. Firepower
8. Firehouse
9. Firefight
10. Fireguard
11. Firewater
12. Fireflood
13. Firestorm
14. Firebrand
15. Fireproof
16. Firebrick
17. Firedrake
18. Firetruck

6
1. Hairdo
2. Hairnet
3. haircap
4. hairpin
5. haircut
6. hairband
7. hairline
8. hairlike
9. hairlock
10. hairless
11. hairworm
12. hairball
13. Hairwork
14. Hairpiece
15. Hairstyle
16. Haircloth
17. Hairspray
18. Hairbrush

7
1. Paintball
2. Dodgeball
3. Blackball
4. Slimeball
5. Wallyball
6. Beachball
7. Screwball
8. Roundball
9. Stickball
10. Broomball
11. Stoopball
12. Curveball
13. Trackball
14. Buckyball
15. Speedball
16. Scuzzball
17. punchball
18. Eightball

8
1. Malevolent
2. Sinister
3. Wicked
4. Malicious
5. Cruel
6. Diabolical
7. Vile
8. Corrupt
9. Dark
10. Maleficent
11. Villainous
12. Malignant
13. Nefarious
14. Depraved
15. Iniquitous

9
1. Fuzz
2. Buzz
3. Jazz
4. Razz
5. Fizz
6. Scuzz
7. Spazz
8. Frizz
9. Whizz
10. Abuzz
11. Pizazz
12. Bezazz
13. Schnozz
14. Razzmatazz

10
1. Whitewash
2. Greenwash
3. Mouthwash
4. Stonewash
5. Brainwash
6. Backwash
7. Flatwash
8. Downwash
9. Rainwash
10. Hogwash
11. Carwash
12. Eyewash
13. Outwash
14. Prewash

FIRSTS 8♦

A	Choose a Question

2	Stephen King's First Novel was published in 1974. Name any of his first 11 novels published under his own name.

3	There are 11 U.N. Member nations whose official name begins with the Letter "G." Name these 11 countries.

4	Name any of the First 10 letters of the Greek Alphabet.

5	Stephen Spielberg has directed over 30 films. His first theatrical release came in 1974. Name any of the first 10 Spielberg Directed films released in theaters.

6	There are 12 NFL teams whose Nickname starts with a letter that is alphabetically before the first letter in their geographic name (city). Name any of these 12 NFL teams

7	There are 12 Elements on the Periodic Table that have the first Letter "C." Name any of these 12 elements.

8	There have been 33 Marvel Cinematic Universe films with plans to exceed 40 by the end of the decade. Name (with Full Name) any of the First 10 MCU films chronologically.

9	American Idol debuted in 2002 and ran for 15 seasons before "going on hiatus" for two years. Name any of the first 15 American Idol Winners.

10	There are 66 books in the King James Bible. Name any of the first 10.

Firsts 8♦

2
1. Carrie
2. Salem's Lot
3. The Shining
4. The Stand
5. The Dead Zone
6. The Mist
7. Firestarter
8. Cujo
9. The Dark Tower: The Gunslinger
10. Christine
11. Pet Sematary

3
1. Gabon
2. Gambia
3. Georgia
4. Germany
5. Ghana
6. Greece
7. Grenada
8. Guatemala
9. Guinea
10. Guinea-Bissau
11. Guyana

4
1. Alpha
2. Beta
3. Gamma
4. Delta
5. Epsilon
6. Zeta
7. Eta
8. Theta
9. Iota
10. Kappa

5
1. The Sugarland Express
2. Jaws
3. Close Encounters of the 3rd Kind
4. 1941
5. Raiders of the Lost Ark
6. ET The Extra-Terrestrial
7. Twilight Zone: The Movie
8. Indiana Jones & The Temple of Doom
9. The Color Purple
10. Empire of the Sun

6
1. Cincinnati Bengals
2. Cleveland Browns
3. Dallas Cowboys
4. Denver Broncos
5. Indianapolis Colts
6. Kansas City Chiefs
7. Miami Dolphins
8. New York Giants
9. Philadelphia Eagles
10. San Francisco 49ers
11. Tampa Bay Buccaneers
12. Washington Commanders

7
1. Cadmium
2. Casesium
3. Calcium
4. Californium
5. Carbon
6. Cerium
7. Chlorine
8. Chromium
9. Cobalt
10. Copernicium
11. Copper
12. Curium

8
1. Iron Man
2. The Incredible Hulk
3. Iron Man 2
4. Thor
5. Captain America: First Avenger
6. The Avengers
7. Iron Man 3
8. Thor: The Dark World
9. Captain America: Winter Soldier
10. Guardians of the Galaxy

9
1. Kelly Clarkson
2. Ruben Studdard
3. Fantasia Barrino
4. Carrie Underwood
5. Taylor Hicks
6. Jordin Sparks
7. David Cook
8. Kris Allen
9. Lee DeWyze
10. Scotty McCreery
11. Phillip Phillips
12. Candice Glover
13. Caleb Johnson
14. Nick Fradini
15. Trent Harmon

10
1. Genesis
2. Exodus
3. Leviticus
4. Numbers
5. Deuteronomy
6. Joshua
7. Judges
8. Ruth
9. 1 Samuel
10. 2 Samual

FOOTBALL 9♦

A	Choose a Question

2	The University of Minnesota plays football in the Big 10 College Football Conference as the Golden Gophers. Name any other of the other 13 football team nicknames among the Big 10.

3	12 NFL Quarterbacks have led their team to a Super Bowl Victory more than one time. Name the QBs with 2 or more Super Bowl victories.

4	With the 2023 Super Bowl, the Kansas City Chiefs joined 11 other NFL teams on the list of teams to appear in 5 or more Super Bowls. Name those 11 NFL Teams

5	In Jan 2023, Georgia defeated TCU to win the 9th College Football National Championship. TCU is only the 14th team to even be invited to this competition. Name the other 12 Schools who have played in a CFP game prior to Jan 2023

6	Tom Brady leads all NFL Quarterbacks with 89,215 career passing yards, 11 other NFL QBs have reached the 50,000 yard milestone. Name them.

7	The Steelers and the Patriots have each won 6 Super Bowls. On the other hand, 12 teams have never won a Super Bowl, 4 never even have played in one. Name any of these 12 NFL teams that never won this Championship Game.

8	College Football has been naming champions since 1869. In those 150+ years 14 colleges lay claim to 6 or more "National Championships." Name them

9	11 Current NFL Franchises have been playing Football since the 1940s. Name any of the 11 oldest NFL Franchises

10	29% of the NFL's Super Bowls have been played in the State of Florida. Counting the upcoming 2024 location, Name any of the 13 Metro Areas outside of Florida that have been named hosts of the NFL's ultimate game.

FOOTBALL - 9♦

2
1. Fighting Illini (Illinois)
2. Hoosiers (Indiana)
3. Hawkeyes (Iowa)
4. Terrapins (Maryland)
5. Spartans (Michigan State)
6. Wolverines (Michigan)
7. Cornhuskers (Nebraska)
8. Wildcats (Northwestern)
9. Buckeyes (Ohio State)
10. Nittany Lions (Penn State)
11. Boilermakers (Purdue)
12. Scarlet Knights (Rutgers)
13. Badgers (Wisconsin)

3
1. Peyton Manning
2. Eli Manning
3. Jim Plunkett
4. Bart Starr
5. Ben Roethlisberger
6. Bob Greise
7. Roger Staubach
8. John Elway
9. Troy Aikman
10. John Elway
11. Terry Bradshaw
12. Tom Brady

4
1. New England Patriots
2. Pittsburgh Steelers
3. Dallas Cowboys
4. Denver Broncos
5. San Francisco 49ers
6. Green Bay Packers
7. New York Giants
8. Washington Redskins/ Commanders
9. Oakland/LA/
10. Las Vegas Raiders
11. Miami Dolphins

5
1. Alabama
2. LSU
3. Ohio State
4. Michigan
5. Michigan State
6. Oregon
7. Washington
8. Clemson
9. Notre Dame
10. Oklahoma
11. Cincinnati
12. Florida State

6
1. Tom Brady
2. Drew Brees
3. Peyton Manning
4. Brett Favre
5. Ben Roethlisberger
6. Phillip Rivers
7. Matt Ryan
8. Dan Marino
9. Aaron Rodgers
10. Eli Manning
11. Matthew Stafford
12. John Elway

7
1. Buffalo Bills
2. Minnesota Vikings
3. Cincinnati Bengals
4. Atlanta Falcons
5. Carolina Panthers
6. Tennessee Titans
7. Los Angeles Chargers
8. Arizona Cardinals
9. Cleveland Browns
10. Detroit Lions
11. Houston Texans
12. Jacksonville Jaguars

8
1. Princeton
2. Yale
3. Alabama
4. Michigan
5. Notre Dame
6. Southern California (USC)
7. Pittsburgh
8. Ohio State
9. Harvard
10. Minnesota
11. Oklahoma
12. Pennsylvania
13. Michigan State
14. Tennessee

9
1. Arizona Cardinals
2. Chicago Bears
3. Green Bay Packers
4. New York Giants
5. Detroit Lions
6. Washington Commanders
7. Pittsburgh Steelers
8. Philadelphia Eagles
9. Los Angeles Rams
10. Cleveland Browns
11. San Francisco 49ers

10
1. Minneapolis
2. New York
3. Detroit
4. Atlanta
5. Indianapolis
6. New Orleans
7. Dallas
8. Houston
9. Phoenix
10. San Diego
11. Los Angeles
12. San Francisco
13. Las Vegas

GOLF & TENNIS 10♦

A	Choose a Question

2	Donald Trump owns 16 golf courses, 4 International, 12 in the USA. They are mostly named after him and the city in which it resides. Name any of the 16 cities where a Trump Golf course is located.

3	Starting in 1972, The Davis Cup has been the Premier Men's Team Tennis Championship. The United States leads all nations with 9 wins, Name the other 15 Nations that have won.

4	The 4 Major Tournaments that make up the Grand Slam of Tennis have been won by 15 Tennis Players 10 times or more. Name these 15 most tournament winning male or female Tennis players.

5	14 U.S. Tennis Players (6 Men, 8 Women) have been ranked for at least a week as the #1 Tennis player in the world by either the ATP or WTA. Name them

6	According to Box Office Mojo, only 10 movies about Tennis or Golf made $10 million or more at the box office. Name these 10 films.

7	There have been 14 Men's Golfers who have won 6 or more Majors in Professional Golfing, with one having as many as 18. Name them

8	In the 42 years from 1981 to 2022, Wimbledon's Gentlemen's Singles Tournament has been won by only 15 different Men's tennis players. Name any of these 15 Wimbledon Men's Singles Tournament winners

9	Bleacher Report's Golf Writer listed the 10 Golf Tournaments Every Hardcore Fan needs to attend in a 2012 article. Name these courses

10	The USA leads the world in number of Golf Courses with over 16,000, 10,000 more than the #2 nation. Ireland is #14 with 365. Name the 12 Nations with the most Golf Courses in between.

GOLF & TENNIS 10◆

2
1. Dubai, UAE
2. Doonbeg, Ireland
3. Aberdeen, Scotland
4. Turnberry, Scotland
5. New York, NY
6. Westchester, NY
7. Hudson Valley, NY
8. West Palm Beach, FL
9. Miami, FL
10. Jupiter, FL
11. Bedminster, NJ
12. Colts Neck, NJ
13. Washington, DC
14. Philadelphia, PA
15. Los Angeles, CA
16. Charlotte, NC

3
1. Sweden
2. Australia
3. Spain
4. France
5. Germany
6. Czech Republic
7. Russia
8. Croatia
9. South Africa
10. Italy
11. Serbia
12. Switzerland
13. Great Britain
14. Argentina
15. Canada

4
1. Margaret Court
2. Novak Djokovic
3. Serena Williams
4. Steffi Graf
5. Rafael Nadal
6. Roger Federer
7. Helen Wills Moody
8. Chris Evert
9. Martina Navratilova
10. Pete Sampras
11. Roy Emerson
12. Billie Jean King
13. Rod Laver
14. Bjorn Borg
15. Bill Tilden

5
1. Andre Agassi
2. Jimmy Connors
3. Jim Courier
4. John McEnroe
5. Andy Roddick
6. Pete Sampras

7. Tracy Austin
8. Jennifer Capriati
9. Lindsay Davenport
10. Chris Evert
11. Martina Navratilova
12. Monica Seles
13. Serena Williams
14. Venus WIlliams

6
1. Tin Cup
2. Caddyshack
3. King Richard
4. Wimbledon
5. Happy Gilmore
6. Legend of Bagger Vance
7. Battle of the Sexes
8. The Greatest Game Ever Played
9. Caddyshack II
10. Who's Your Caddy?

7
1. Jack Nicklaus
2. Tiger Woods
3. Walter Hagen
4. Ben Hogan
5. Gary Player
6. Tom Watson
7. Harry Vardon
8. Bobby Jones
9. Gene Sarazen
10. Sam Snead
11. Arnold Palmer
12. Lee Trevino
13. Nick Faldo
14. Phil Mickelson

8
1. Novak Djokovic
2. Roger Federer
3. Andy Murray
4. Rafael Nadal
5. Lleyton Hewit
6. Goran Ivanesivic
7. Pete Sampras
8. Richard Krajicek
9. Andre Agassi
10. Michael Stich
11. Stefan Edberg
12. Boris Becker
13. Pat Cash
14. John McEnroe
15. Jimmy Connors

9
1. The Masters
2. AT&T Pebble Beach Pro-Am
3. U.S. Open
4. British Open (St. Andrews)
5. The Players Championship at Sawgrass
6. The Memorial Tournament
7. Farmers Insurance Open at Torrey Pines
8. AT&T National
9. Hyundai Tournament of Champions (Kapalua, HI)
10. Wells Fargo Championship at Quail Hollow

10
1. Japan
2. UK
3. Canada
4. Australia
5. Germany
6. France
7. South Korea
8. Sweden
9. China
10. Spain
11. South Africa
12. New Zealand

HODGE PODGE J♦

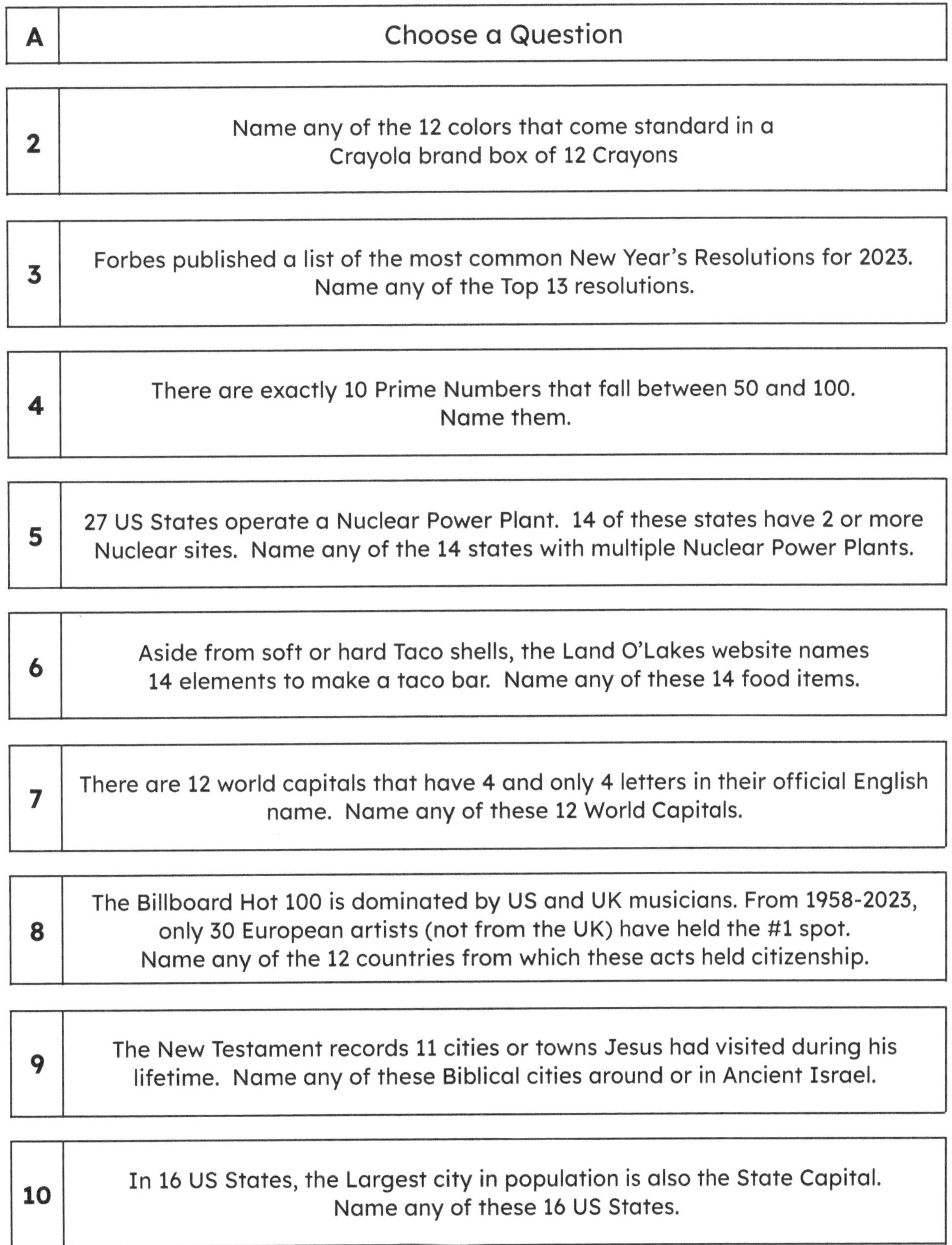

A	Choose a Question

2	Name any of the 12 colors that come standard in a Crayola brand box of 12 Crayons

3	Forbes published a list of the most common New Year's Resolutions for 2023. Name any of the Top 13 resolutions.

4	There are exactly 10 Prime Numbers that fall between 50 and 100. Name them.

5	27 US States operate a Nuclear Power Plant. 14 of these states have 2 or more Nuclear sites. Name any of the 14 states with multiple Nuclear Power Plants.

6	Aside from soft or hard Taco shells, the Land O'Lakes website names 14 elements to make a taco bar. Name any of these 14 food items.

7	There are 12 world capitals that have 4 and only 4 letters in their official English name. Name any of these 12 World Capitals.

8	The Billboard Hot 100 is dominated by US and UK musicians. From 1958-2023, only 30 European artists (not from the UK) have held the #1 spot. Name any of the 12 countries from which these acts held citizenship.

9	The New Testament records 11 cities or towns Jesus had visited during his lifetime. Name any of these Biblical cities around or in Ancient Israel.

10	In 16 US States, the Largest city in population is also the State Capital. Name any of these 16 US States.

HODGE PODGE J♦

2
1. Red
2. Blue
3. Yellow
4. Orange
5. Green
6. VIolet (purple)
7. Brown
8. Black
9. White
10. Gray
11. Carnation Pink
12. Indigo

3
1. Improve Mental Health
2. Lose Weight
3. Improve Fitness
4. Improve Diet
5. Improve Finances
6. Make more time for loved ones
7. Stop Smoking
8. Learn a New Skill
9. Improve Work-Life Balance
10. Meditate Regularly
11. Make more time for Hobbies
12. Travel more
13. Drink Less Alcohol

4
1. 53
2. 59
3. 61
4. 67
5. 71
6. 73
7. 79
8. 83
9. 89
10. 97

5
1. Ground Beef
2. Shredded Beef
3. Chicken
4. Fish
5. Black Beans
6. Salsa
7. Cheese
8. Tomatoes
9. Lettuce
10. Guacamole/Avocado
11. Refried Beans
12. Cilantro
13. Green Onions
14. Sour Cream

6
1. Illinois
2. South Carolina
3. North Carolina
4. Pennsylvania
5. Alabama
6. Florida
7. Louisiana
8. Michigan
9. Minnesota
10. New York
11. Ohio
12. Tennessee
13. Texas
14. Virginia

7
1. Apia
2. Baku
3. Bern
4. Doha
5. Dili
6. Juba
7. Kiev
8. Lome
9. Male
10. Riga
11. Rome
12. Suva

8
1. Sweden
2. France
3. Germany
4. Ireland
5. Netherlands
6. Spain
7. Belgium
8. Austria
9. Czechia
10. Greece
11. Italy
12. Norway

9
1. Bethlehem
2. Nazareth
3. Cana
4. Capernaum
5. Jerusalem
6. Sychar
7. Bethsaida
8. Tyre
9. Sidon
10. Caesera Phillipi
11. Jericho

10
1. Arizona
2. Ohio
3. Indiana
4. Colorado
5. Oklahoma
6. Tennessee
7. Boston
8. Georgia
9. Hawaii
10. Boise
11. Iowa
12. Utah
13. Arkansas
14. Rhode Island
15. West Virginia
16. Wyoming

HOME IMPROVEMENT Q♦

A	Choose a Question

2	Online Polling Site Ranker.Com has a poll for "Best Home Improvement TV Show." Judd Nelson's "Home Time" comes in at #13. Name any of the 12 most popular home improvement shows.

3	According to a Home Depot Video on "Types of Windows," a house can have one of 10 types of Windows. Name any of these 10 window "styles."

4	Bob Vila posted a list of 11 items one should have in a "Basic" Tool kit. Name any of these Hand tools or items.

5	Redfin, a real estate site, lists the 13 most popular styles of house based on list to sell ratios. #13 is the townhouse. Name any of the 12 more popular architectural styles for homes in America.

6	Homebuilding and Renovating.com, in their article, "Types of Flooring: What's best for you," lists 15 different types of floor surfaces for one's home. Name any of these 14 Flooring options

7	In Sept 2022, Forbes published an article detailing the most expensive states in the US to buy a home. Name any of the top 15 most expensive states to live in terms of Average Home prices.

8	Bob Vila lists 15 types of Wood (based on type of Tree) every Do-it-Yourselfer must know. Name any of these 15 types of Woods (or Trees)

9	According to a 2022 survey of leading hardware stores, the 16th most purchased items are plumbing supplies. Name any of the 15 most purchased items from Hardware stores (in volume, not dollar value)

10	According to their own website, Home Depot has 2,298 stores in the USA. 11 states have fewer than 10 stores, name these states

HOME IMPROVEMENT Q♦

2
1. Home Town
2. This Old House
3. Holmes on Homes
4. Fixer Upper
5. Ask this Old House
6. New Yankee Workshop
7. Good Bones
8. Property Brothers
9. Rehab addict
10. Yard Crashers
11. Holmes: Next Generation
12. Love it or List it

3
1. Casement
2. Single Hung
3. Double Hung
4. Bay
5. Sliding
6. Awning
7. Picture
8. Shaped
9. Basement
10. Glass Block

4
1. Screwdriver set
2. Tape Measure
3. Toolbox
4. Hammer
5. Duct Tape
6. Flashlight
7. Set of Pliers
8. Utility Knife
9. Putty Knife
10. Handsaw
11. Adjustable Wrench

5
1. Ranch
2. Craftsman
3. Colonial
4. Cape Cod
5. Tudor
6. Victorian
7. Mediterranean
8. Modern
9. Contemporary
10. Cottage
11. Farmhouse
12. Mid-Century Modern

6
1. Stone
2. Porcelain Tile
3. Wood
4. Ceramic
5. Solid (Hard) Wood
6. Engineered Wood
7. Linoleum
8. Vinyl
9. Carpet
10. Concrete
11. Cork
12. Bamboo
13. Laminate
14. Leather Tiles
15. Rubber

7
1. Hawaii
2. California
3. New York
4. Washington
5. Massachusetts
6. Colorado
7. Oregon
8. Utah
9. New Jersey
10. Rhode Island
11. Maryland
12. Alaska
13. Connecticut
14. Virginia
15. Wyoming

8
1. Cedar
2. Fir
3. Pine
4. Redwood
5. Ash
6. Birch
7. Cherry
8. Mahogany
9. Maple
10. Oak
11. Poplar
12. Teak
13. Walnut
14. Acacia
15. Beech

9
1. Adhesives (Glues)
2. Work/Latex Gloves
3. Wrenches
4. Tapes
5. Keys/Door Locks
6. Light Bulbs
7. Fasteners (Screws/Nails)
8. Batteries
9. Washers (not for clothes)
10. Hinges
11. Latches
12. Handles/Door Handles
13. Wires & Ropes
14. Chains
15. Belts

10
1. South Dakota
2. North Dakota
3. Vermont
4. Wyoming
5. Montana
6. West Virginia
7. Alaska
8. Hawaii
9. Nebraska
10. Rhode Island
11. Delaware

JUNK FOOD K♦

A	Choose a Question

2	The Pop Tarts Website lists 15 flavors of Pop Tarts under their "Favorites" Banner (excludes limited editions). Without regard to their Frosting (or lack thereof), Name any of the 15 Classic Pop Tart flavors.

3	Potato Chips go with Dip. Dean Foods makes 13 flavors of Chip Dip, counting the 6 in its' Sports Bar Favorites line. Name any of these 13 Dean's Flavors.

4	Little Debbie has licensed Hudsonville Ice Cream to make Flavors inspired by the more popular Little Debbie snack Products. Name any of these 11 Little Debbie Ice Cream Pints

5	In 2022, Shane Co released an infographic detailing the most popular chip in every state based on google search and analytics. 17 brands could claim the top spot in at least one state. Name any of these 17 popular chip brands.

6	There are 12 items you can order to eat on the standard everyday McDonald's menu that they have registered trademarks on (some have multiple types). Name them

7	In 2012, Time Magazine published an article naming the "Top 10 most iconic Junk foods." Name any of these 10 brands or types.

8	Dippin Dots, the flash frozen in Liquid Nitrogen Ice Cream, has 11 flavors for sale from its online store. Name any of these 11 ice cream flavors

9	In 2023, Parade magazine ranked all 30 flavors of Pringles Potato Chips. Name any of the flavors that were in the top 12

10	In 2021, A dozen Fast Food Burger Joints showed over $1 Billion in sales across all restaurants. Name any of these 12 most popular Fast Food Burger Places.

Junk Food K♦

2
1. Blueberry
2. Cinnamon Brown Sugar
3. Cherry
4. Chocolate Chip
5. Chocolate Fudge
6. Confetti
7. Cookies & Cream
8. Grape
9. Hot Fudge Sundae
10. Eggo Maple
11. Raspberry
12. Smores
13. Strawberry
14. Wildlicious Wild Berry
15. Snickerdoodle

3
1. French Onion
2. Ranch
3. Guacamole
4. Cheddar Bacon
5. French Onion With Bacon
6. Bacon Ranch
7. Veggie
8. Nacho Cheese
9. Loaded Potato Skins
10. Buffalo Wing
11. Deep Fried Pickle
12. Nashville Hot
13. Pepperoni Pizza

4
1. Birthday Cakes
2. Cosmic Brownies
3. Fudge Rounds
4. Honey Buns
5. Nutty Buddy
6. Oatmeal Creme Pies
7. Star Crunch
8. Strawberry Shortcake Rolls
9. Swiss Rolls
10. Unicorn Cakes
11. Zebra Cakes

5
1. Pringles
2. Sun Chips
3. Tostitos
4. Doritos
5. Cheetos
6. Funyuns
7. Popchips
8. Miss Vickie's
9. Lays
10. Bugles
11. Zapp's
12. Cape Cod
13. Utz
14. Old Dutch
15. Ruffles
16. Fritos
17. Takis

6
1. Big Mac
2. Quarter Pounder
3. McDouble
4. Filet-O-Fish
5. McChicken
6. McCrispy
7. McMuffin
8. Big Breakfast
9. McNuggets
10. McFlurry
11. World Famous Fries
12. Happy Meal

7
1. Twinkie
2. Cheese Puffs
3. Moon Pies
4. Doughnuts
5. McDonald's French Fries
6. Chipwich
7. Pork Rinds
8. Snickers
9. Pepperoni Pizza
10. Doritos

8
1. Banana Split
2. Birthday Cake
3. Chocolate Chip Cookie Dough
4. Brownie Batter
5. Cookies N Cream
6. Cool Mint Crunch
7. Cotton Candy
8. Spookies N Cream
9. Strawberry
10. Vanilla
11. Chocolate

9
1. Pizza
2. Extreme Screamin Dill Pickle
3. BBQ
4. Buffalo Ranch
5. Cheddar & Sour Cream
6. Original
7. Salt & Vinegar
8. Sour Cream & Onion
9. French Onion Dip
10. Wavy Original
11. Ranch
12. Cheddar Cheese

10
1. McDonald's
2. Wendy's
3. Burger King
4. Sonic Drive-In
5. Dairy Queen
6. Jack in the Box
7. Whataburger
8. Culver's
9. Hardee's
10. Five Guys
11. Carl's Jr.
12. In-N-Out Burger

KID'S STUFF A♥

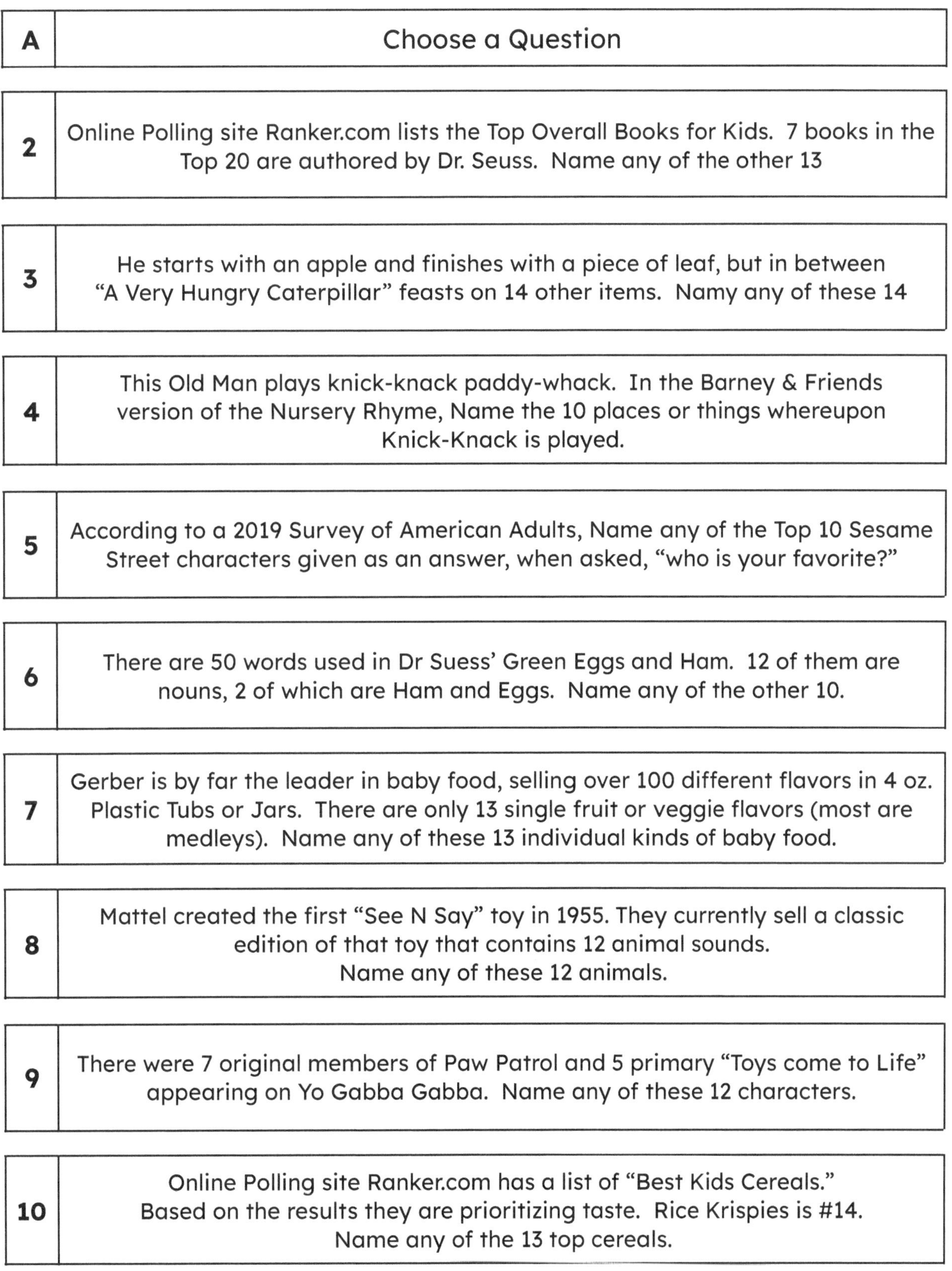

A	Choose a Question
2	Online Polling site Ranker.com lists the Top Overall Books for Kids. 7 books in the Top 20 are authored by Dr. Seuss. Name any of the other 13
3	He starts with an apple and finishes with a piece of leaf, but in between "A Very Hungry Caterpillar" feasts on 14 other items. Namy any of these 14
4	This Old Man plays knick-knack paddy-whack. In the Barney & Friends version of the Nursery Rhyme, Name the 10 places or things whereupon Knick-Knack is played.
5	According to a 2019 Survey of American Adults, Name any of the Top 10 Sesame Street characters given as an answer, when asked, "who is your favorite?"
6	There are 50 words used in Dr Suess' Green Eggs and Ham. 12 of them are nouns, 2 of which are Ham and Eggs. Name any of the other 10.
7	Gerber is by far the leader in baby food, selling over 100 different flavors in 4 oz. Plastic Tubs or Jars. There are only 13 single fruit or veggie flavors (most are medleys). Name any of these 13 individual kinds of baby food.
8	Mattel created the first "See N Say" toy in 1955. They currently sell a classic edition of that toy that contains 12 animal sounds. Name any of these 12 animals.
9	There were 7 original members of Paw Patrol and 5 primary "Toys come to Life" appearing on Yo Gabba Gabba. Name any of these 12 characters.
10	Online Polling site Ranker.com has a list of "Best Kids Cereals." Based on the results they are prioritizing taste. Rice Krispies is #14. Name any of the 13 top cereals.

Kid's Stuff A♥

2
1. Charlie and the Chocolate Factory
2. Where the Wild Things Are
3. Charlotte's Web
4. Goodnight Moon
5. Where the Sidewalk Ends
6. Matilda
7. If You Give a Mouse a Cookie (Laura Numeroff)
8. Clifford the Big Red Dog
9. The Complete Tales of Winnie the Pooh
10. Corduroy (Don Freeman)
11. Three Little Pigs
12. James and the Giant Peach
13. The Lion, The WItch, and The Wardrobe

3
1. Pears
2. Plums
3. Strawberries
4. Oranges
5. Chocolate Cake
6. Strawberry Ice Cream Cone
7. Pickle
8. Swiss Cheese
9. Salami
10. Lollipop
11. Cherry Pie
12. Sausage
13. Cupcake
14. Watermelon

4
1. 1 thumb
2. 2 Shoe
3. 3 Knee
4. 4 door
5. 5 Hive
6. 6 Sticks
7. 7 Heaven (up in)
8. 8 Gate
9. 9 Spine
10. 10. shin

r

5
1. Cookie Monster
2. Elmo
3. Big Bird
4. Oscar the Grouch
5. Grover
6. Count von Count
7. Snuffleupagus
8. Ernie
9. Bert
10. Abby Cadabby

6
1. boat
2. box
3. car
4. fox
5. goat
6. house
7. mouse
8. rain
9. train
10. tree

7
1. Banana
2. Carrot
3. Apple
4. Pear
5. Pea
6. Sweet potato
7. Butternut Squash
8. Green Bean
9. Mango
10. Corn
11. Prune
12. Peach
13. Pumpkin

8
1. Bird
2. Cat
3. Cow
4. Coyote
5. Dog
6. Duck
7. Frog
8. Horse
9. Pig
10. Rooster
11. Sheep
12. Turkey

9
1. Ryder
2. Chase
3. Marshall
4. Sky
5. Rocky
6. Rubble
7. Zuma

8. Muno
9. Foofa
10. Plex
11. Brobee
12. Toodee

10
1. Cap'n Crunch
2. Cinnamon Toast Crunch
3. Froot Loops
4. Lucky Charms
5. Frosted Flakes
6. Fruity Pebbles
7. Honey Nut Cheerios
8. Cocoa Pebbles
9. Cocoa Puffs
10. Apple Jacks
11. Trix
12. Corn Pops
13. Cookie Crisp

MUSIC 2♥

A	Choose a Question
2	Online Polling Site Ranker asked the question, "What are the best Musical Duos of all time." 13 of the Top 15 were acts that performed as two people. Name any of these Top 13 favorite Duos of All Time.
3	Billboard has a list of the 20 best performances of Songs by Women. 14 of these songs are by women as solo artists. Name any of these 14 all time great songs by women.
4	Huey Lewis & the News' 3rd Single from 1984's Sports was "The Heart of Rock and Roll," which specifically names 13 Cities where the Heart is "still beating." Name any of these 13 US Cities.
5	In 1984, Band-Aid recorded "We are the World." 37 singers representing 15 bands sung on the single. Name any of these 15 Bands.
6	Katy Perry had 5 US #1's from one album, and 14 Top 10 hits overall. Name any of these 14 Chart Topping Katy Perry songs.
7	Lonely Planet's Travel suggestions for a "Rock N Roll" destination range from Joshua Tree to Billy Joel's Italian Restaurant; Some obvious, some less so. Name any of the 13 US cities these Rock destinations lie in or very near.
8	A Supergroup is a band formed with members of previously successful bands. According to online polling site Ranker.com. Sammy Hagar's Chickenfoot ranks #16. Name any of the 15 supergroups ranked ahead of them.
9	Bon Jovi had their first Top 40 hit in 1984, their last one in 1995. All told they had 14 Top 40 hits. Name any of these 14 Bon Jovi Songs.
10	In June 2023, Billboard put out a list of the 50 Best Rap Groups of All Time. Amazingly, The Beastie Boys are listed #16. Name any of the Rap Groups in the Top 15

MUSIC 2♥

2
1. Righteous Brothers
2. Everly Brothers
3. Simon & Garfunkel
4. Hall & Oates
5. The Carpenters
6. Tears for Fears
7. Eurythmics
8. Outkast
9. Daft Punk
10. White Stripes
11. Sam & Dave
12. Wham
13. Air Supply

3
1. How Do I Live (LeAnn Rimes)
2. Physical (Olivia Newton-John)
3. You Light Up My Life (Debby Boone)
4. We Belong Together (Mariah Carey)
5. Un-Break My Heart (Tony Braxton)
6. Bette Davis Eyes (Kim Carnes)
7. You Were Meant For Me (Jewel)
8. Flashdance...What a Feeling (Irene Cara)
9. Rolling in the Deep (Adele)
10. Call Me Maybe (Carly Rae Jepsen)
11. No One (Alicia Keys)
12. I Will Always Love You (Whitney Houston)
13. TiK ToK (Ke$ha)
14. Royals (Lorde)

4
1. New York
2. Los Angeles (LA)
3. Hollywood
4. San Antonio
5. Boston
6. Baton Rouge
7. Tulsa
8. Austin
9. Oklahoma City
10. Seattle
11. San Francisco
12. Cleveland
13. Detroit

5
1. Kool & the Gang
2. U2
3. Boomtown Rats
4. Genesis
5. Ultravox
6. Bananarama
7. Culture Club
8. Heaven 17
9. Spandau Ballet
10. Duran Duran
11. Wham!
12. Status Quo
13. The Police
14. Shalamar
15. The Style Council

6
1. I Kissed a Girl
2. Hot N Cold
3. Waking Up in Vegas
4. California Gurls
5. Teenage Dream
6. Firework
7. E.T.
8. Last Friday Night (TGIF)
9. The One that Got Away
10. Part of Me
11. Wide Awake
12. Roar
13. Dark Horse
14. Chained to the Rhythm

7
1. St Louis, MO
2. Cleveland, OH
3. Memphis, TN
4. Clarksdale, MS
5. New York, NY
6. Los Angeles, CA
7. Lubbock, TX
8. Seattle, WA
9. Chicago, IL
10. San Francisco, CA
11. Bethel (Woodstock), NY
12. Mason City, IA
13. Belmar, NJ

8
1. Traveling Wilburys
2. Cream
3. Crosby, Stills, Nash & Young
4. The Highwaymen
5. Blind Faith
6. Derek & the Dominos
7. Bad Company
8. Journey
9. Emerson Lake & Palmer
10. Audioslave
11. The HoneyDrippers
12. The Dirty Mac
13. Temple of the Dog
14. Asia
15. Foo Fighters

9
1. Runaway
2. You Give Love a Bad Name
3. Livin' On A Prayer
4. Wanted Dead or Alive
5. Bad Medicine
6. Born to Be My Baby
7. I'll Be There for You
8. Lay Your Hands on Me
9. Living in Sin
10. Keep The Faith
11. Bed of Roses
12. In These Arms
13. Always
14. This Ain't A Love Song

10
1. Naughty By Nature
2. Fugees
3. Mobb Deep
4. Grandmaster Flash & the Furious Five
5. Migos
6. The Roots
7. De La Soul
8. Salt-N-Pepa
9. Eric B & Rakim
10. Public Enemy
11. Run-D.M.C.
12. A Tribe Called Quest
13. N.W.A
14. Wu-Tang Clan
15. OutKast

Music: Deep Cuts 3♥

A	Choose a Question
2	The Rock and Roll Hall of Fame has inducted 15 groups that include at least one set of brothers. Name any of these 15 "Rock and Roll" groups.
3	As of July 2023, 20 Musical Artists or Bands have had songs at #1 on the Billboard Hot 100 for 12 weeks or more. Name any of these 12 performers.
4	In 2022, Guitar World conducted a reader survey asking for the greatest guitar solos of all time. Name any of the 15 virtuoso guitarists whose Guitar solos made the top 15.
5	14 Albums have stayed in the Billboard top 200 Albums for 10 years or more. 6 of these albums are of the "Greatest Hits" variety. Name the 14 Music groups or Artists who created these albums.
6	Rolling Stone Magazine published a list of the 100 greatest drummers of all time in 2016. Name any of the 16 drummers that made the top 15. (2 drummers from the same band were listed at #6)
7	"People Get Ready/One Love" is the first track on Side 2 of Legend, the Bob Marley Greatest Hits Compilation. Name any of the other 13 other songs
8	Elvis has a greatest hits album called called "30 #1 Hits." 18 of these #1's are on the US pop charts. Name any of these 18 songs.
9	When MTV debuted in 1981, 17 of the first 50 videos featured Bands or Individuals that would be inducted in the Rock and Roll Hall of Fame by 2023. Name any of these 17 artists and video pioneers.
10	In 2018, Playbill published an article listing the top selling Musical Cast Albums of all time. Name the 15 Broadway shows that produced albums at the top of this list

MUSIC: DEEP CUTS 3♥

2
1. Everly Brothers
2. Beach Boys
3. The Kinks
4. The Isley Brothers
5. CCR
6. Sly and the Family Stone
7. Allman Brothers
8. Bee Gees
9. Jackson 5
10. Earth Wind & Fire
11. Grandmaster Flash & the Furious Five
12. Van Halen
13. The Stooges
14. Dire Straits
15. Radiohead

3
1. Lil Nas X
2. Mariah Carey & Boyz II Men
3. Luis Fonsi & Daddy Yankee
4. Harry Styles
5. Whitney Houston
6. Boyz II Men
7. Los Del Rio
8. Elton John
9. Mariah Carey
10. Black Eyed Peas
11. Mark Ronson
12. Morgan Wallen
13. Brandy & Monica
14. Santana
15. Eminem
16. Usher
17. Robin Thicke
18. Wiz Khalifa
19. Chainsmokers
20. Ed Sheeran

4
1. Kirk Hammett
2. Eric Clapton
3. Ritchie Blackmore
4. Prince
5. Jimi Hendrix
6. Randy Rhoads
7. Eddie Van Halen
8. Allen Collins
9. Mark Knopfler
10. Slash
11. Don Felder
12. Joe Walsh
13. Jimmy Page
14. David Gilmour
15. Brian May

5
1. Pink Floyd (Dark Side of the Moon)
2. Bob Marley (Legend)
3. Journey (Greatest Hits)
4. Metallica (Metallica)
5. Creedence Clearwater Revival (Chronicle)
6. Eminem (Curtain Call: The Hits)
7. Nirvana (Nevermind)
8. Guns N' Roses (Greatest Hits)
9. Bruno Mars (Doo Wops & Hooligans)
10. Michael Jackson (Thriller)
11. AC/DC (Back In Black)
12. Adele (21)
13. Kendrick Lamar (Good Kid m.A.A.d City)
14. Queen (Greatest Hits)

6
1. John Bonham
2. Keith Moon
3. Ginger Baker
4. Neil Peart
5. Hal Blaine
6. Clyde Stubblefield
7. John "Jabo" Starks
8. Gene Krupa
9. Mitch Mitchell
10. Al Jackson Jr
11. Steward Copeland
12. Benny Benjamin
13. Charlie Watts
14. D.J. Fontana
15. Ringo Starr
16. Buddy Rich

7
1. Is This Love?
2. No Woman, No Cry
3. Could You Be Loved?
4. Three Little Birds
5. Buffalo Soldier
6. Get Up, Stand Up
7. Stir It Up
8. I Shot the Sheriff
9. Waiting in Vain
10. Redemption Song
11. Satisfy My Soul
12. Exodus
13. Jamming

8
1. Heartbreak Hotel
2. I Want You, I Need You, I Love You
3. Hound Dog
4. Don't Be Cruel
5. Love Me Tender
6. Too Much
7. All Shook Up
8. (Let Me Be Your) Teddy Bear
9. Jailhouse Rock
10. Don't
11. Hard Headed Woman
12. A Big Hunk of Love
13. Stuck on You
14. It's Now or Never
15. Are You Lonesome Tonight?
16. Surrender
17. Good Luck Charm
18. Suspicious Minds

9
1. Pat Benatar
2. Rod Stewart
3. The Who
4. The Pretenders
5. Todd Rundgren
6. The Cars
7. Phil Collins
8. Stevie Nicks
9. Tom Petty and the Heartbreakers
10. Carly Simon
11. Elvis Costello
12. Robert Plant
13. Fleetwood Mac
14. Blondie
15. Kate Bush
16. David Bowie
17. Talking Heads

10
1. Hamilton
2. Les Miserables
3. Phantom of the Opera
4. My Fair Lady
5. Wicked
6. Rent
7. A Chorus Line
8. Fiddler on the Roof
9. Jersey Boys
10. The Lion King
11. Mamma Mia!
12. Miss Saigon
13. The Music Man
14. Cats
15. Evita

PAIRED QUESTIONS 4♥

A	Choose a Question

2	There are 7 John Travolta films with memorable dance sequences, Olivia Newton John had 5 US Billboard #1 hits. Name any of these 12 Movies or Songs.

3	One Kid's TV show had a fictional 5 member band known as "The Zack Attack." Another kid's show had a 6 piece group known as "The Silver Platters" Give the first and last names of any of the characters in these music groups.

4	There are 5 US state capitals that begin with the Letter A. There are 5 countries in Europe whose names end in -Land. Name any of these 10 capital cities or European Countries.

5	There are 6 types of Triangles that Geometry gives specific names. Also, there are 6 four sided objects that have specific names. Name any of these 12 geometric terms

6	5 Steven Spielberg Films have starred Tom Hanks. 7 Live action Tim Burton Films have featured Johnny Depp. Name any of these 12 Movies.

7	Cincinnati's Skyline Restaurant's most famous dish served "5-way" has 5 ingredients. Also, there are 5 brands of Toilet paper with 5 star reviews on Amazon. Name any of the 10 ingredients or brands of toilet tissue

8	There are 5 Boroughs of New York City. Yugoslavia was broken up in 1992 and now contains 7 recognized successor states. Name any of these 12 locations

9	There are 4 states of Matter. There are 6 ways to score on the Bottom Half of a Yahtzee scorecard (besides Yahtzee). Give these 10 answers.

10	In Tetris, there are 7 blocks named after the Letter of the Alphabet they resemble. There are 5 building blocks of DNA or RNA normally denoted by a single letter. Name any of these 11 Letters (one overlaps)

Paired Questions 4♥

2
1. Grease
2. Hairspray
3. Michael
4. Pulp Fiction
5. Saturday Night Fever
6. Staying Alive
7. Urban Cowboy

8. I Honestly Love You
9. Have You Never Been Mellow
10. You're the One that I Want
11. Magic
12. Physical

3
1. Zack Morris
2. Jessica Spano
3. AC Slater
4. Sam "Screech" Powers
5. Lisa Turtle

6. Greg Brady
7. Marcia Brady
8. Peter Brady
9. Jan Brady
10. Bobby Brady
11. Cyndy Brady

4
1. Albany
2. Annapolis
3. Atlanta
4. Augusta
5. Austin

6. Poland
7. Switzerland
8. Finland
9. Iceland
10. Ireland

5
1. Acute
2. Obtuse
3. Right
4. Isosceles
5. Equilateral
6. Scalene

7. Square
8. Parallelogram
9. Rectangle
10. Rhombus
11. Trapezoid
12. Kite

6
1. Saving Private Ryan
2. Catch Me If you Can
3. The Terminal
4. Bridge of Spies
5. The Post

6. Dark Shadows
7. Alice in Wonderland
8. Charlie and the Chocolate Factory
9. Sleepy Hollow
10. Sweeney Todd: The Demon Barber of Fleet Street
11. Ed Wood
12. Edward Scissorhands

7
1. Spaghetti
2. Chili
3. Onions
4. Beans
5. Cheese

6. Charmin
7. Cottonelle
8. Angelsoft
9. Quilted Northern
10. Kleenex

8
1. The Bronx
2. Manhattan
3. Queens
4. Staten Island
5. Brooklyn

6. Bosnia and Herzegovina
7. Croatia
8. Kosovo
9. Montenegro
10. North Macedonia
11. Serbia
12. Slovenia

9
1. Solid
2. Liquid
3. Gas
4. Plasma

5. 3 of a Kind
6. 4 of a Kind
7. Full House
8. Small Straight
9. Large Straight
10. Chance

10
1. I
2. J
3. L
4. O
5. S
6. T
7. Z

8. A
9. C
10. G
11. T
12. U

PASTICHE 5♥

A	Choose a Question

2	Consider a list of all the US States ranked by number of consonants in its name, from most to least. Name any of the first 11 US States on this list.

3	12 Countries have weapons on their National Flags, with swords and spears being the most common. Name any of the 12 countries whose National Flag bears a weapon.

4	Interstate 90 is America's Longest highway traveling 3,021 miles from Boston to Seattle, passing through 11 other states besides Massachusetts and Washington. Name these 11 States

5	Infinite Body Piercing compiled and published a list of over 9,200 piercings they performed in 2020. Aside from the common earlobe piercing, name any of the 13 other body parts they pierced that year.

6	Ron Howard has had 14 movies make over $100 Million at the Box Office Worldwide, where he was either Producer, Director, or both. Name any of the 14 most successful Ron Howard Films.

7	The Letter "E" appears on 12 of the 16 lettered dice that come with the game Boggle. Name any of the 10 letters that appear on only 2 or 3 game dice.

8	As of 2023, 19 girl groups can claim record sales of greater than 20 million copies. Excluding the 6 Asian groups, Name any of the 13 other best-selling Girl Groups.

9	Canada has 3 territories and 10 provinces. Name any of the 10 provinces of Canada

10	There are exactly 10 U.S. States that have more vowels in their name than consonants. Name these 10 States.

PASTICHE 5♥

2
1. Washington
2. West Virginia
3. Rhode Island
4. Pennsylvania
5. North Carolina
6. South Carolina
7. North Dakota
8. Mississippi
9. Connecticut
10. Massachusetts
11. New Hampshire

3
1. Angola
2. Barbados
3. Bolivia
4. Eswatini
5. Guatemala
6. Haiti
7. Kenya
8. Mozambique
9. Oman
10. Saudi Arabia
11. Sri Lanka
12. Venezuela

4
1. Idaho
2. Montana
3. Wyoming
4. South Dakota
5. Minnesota
6. Wisconsin
7. Illinois
8. Indiana
9. Ohio
10. Pennsylvania
11. New York

5
1. Ear (Other)
2. Nipple
3. Nose (Nostril)
4. Belly Button
5. Female genitals
6. Eyebrow
7. Skin (Surface-Varied)
8. Nose Bridge
9. Male Genitals
10. Tongue
11. Lip
12. Perineum
13. Scrotum

6
1. The DaVinci Code
2. Angels & Demons
3. Solo: A Star Wars Story
4. How the Grinch Stole Christmas
5. Apollo 13
6. A Beautiful Mind
7. Ransom
8. Inferno
9. Backdraft
10. Parenthood
11. Cinderella Man
12. Changeling
13. Cowboys & Aliens
14. Changeling

7
1. D
2. U
3. Y
4. B
5. C
6. G
7. M
8. P
9. F
10. V

8
1. Spice Girls
2. The Supremes
3. The Andrews Sisters
4. TLC
5. Destiny's Child
6. Little Mix
7. Pussycat Dolls
8. Bananarama
9. Pointer Sisters
10. Fifth Harmony
11. The Nolans
12. SWV
13. En Vogue

9
1. Ontario
2. Quebec
3. Nova Scotia
4. New Brunswick
5. Manitoba
6. British Columbia
7. Prince Edward Island
8. Saskatchewan
9. Alberta
10. Newfoundland and Labrador

10
1. Alabama
2. Arizona
3. Georgia
4. Hawaii
5. Idaho
6. Indiana
7. Iowa
8. Louisiana
9. Maine
10. Ohio

PEOPLE (VS. AI) 6♥

A	Choose a Question
2	We asked an AI Chatbot to name some performers or artists that "Died too Young." Name Any of the 15 Actors, Actresses, or Musicians the AI named.
3	An AI Chatbot was asked to name the 12 most notorious murderers in US History. Name any of the 10 men and 2 women the AI named.
4	We asked an AI Chatbot to name the 15 most famous artists that one would classify as painters. Name any of the 15 artists listed
5	Two AI chatbots were asked to name the best stand up comedians in history. Name any of the 15 comedians that were named.
6	In July 2023, we asked an AI Chatbot to name the celebrity couples people want to know about most. Name any of these 12 celebrity couples
7	We asked three AI Chatbots to name the 10 most beloved cartoon characters of all time. Name any of the 16 characters they listed
8	We asked a Chatbot AI to name the worst people to be sat next to on an Airplane flight. Describe the 11 types of passengers the AI named.
9	We asked an AI Chatbot to name the most notorious U.S. mobsters in history. Name any of the 12 gangsters that were named.
10	A Chatbot AI was asked to name the most popular Celebrity TV Chefs people love. Name any of the 12 Chefs the AI listed.

PEOPLE (VS. AI) 6♥

2
1. Kurt Cobain
2. Amy Winehouse
3. Heath Ledger
4. Jimi Hendrix
5. Marilyn Monroe
6. James Dean
7. Aaliyah
8. River Phoenix
9. Janis Joplin
10. Tupac Shakur
11. Judy Garland
12. Selena
13. Quintanilla
14. Jim Morrison
15. Brittany Murphy
16. Brandon Lee

3
1. Charles Manson
2. H.H. Holmes
3. Belle Gunness
4. John Wayne Gacy
5. Jeffrey Dahmer
6. Ted Bundy
7. David Berkowitz (Son of Sam)
8. Richard Ramirez (Night Stalker)
9. Gary Ridgway (Green River Killer)
10. Dennis Rader (BTK Killer)
11. Aileen Wuornos
12. Samuel Little

4
1. Leonardo DaVinci
2. Vincent Van Gogh
3. Pablo Picasso
4. Michelangelo
5. Claude Monet
6. Rembrandt van Rijn
7. Johannes Vermeer
8. Salvador Dali
9. Frida Kahlo
10. Georgia O'Keeffe
11. Edward Hopper
12. Jackson Pollock
13. Gustav Klimt
14. Wassily Kandinsky
15. Andy Warhol

5
1. Richard Pryor
2. George Carlin
3. Eddie Murphy
4. Joan Rivers
5. Robin Williams
6. Chris Rock
7. Bill Hicks
8. Jerry Seinfeld
9. Dave Chappelle
10. Louis C.K.
11. Ellen DeGeneres
12. Bill Burr
13. Steve Martin
14. Groucho Marx
15. Lenny Bruce

6
1. Brad Pitt and Jennifer Aniston
2. Prince Harry and Meghan Markle
3. Kim Kardashian and Kanye West
4. Blake Shelton and Gwen Stefani
5. David Beckham and Victoria Beckham
6. Justin Bieber and Hailey Baldwin
7. Tom Brady and Gisele Bündchen
8. Beyoncé and Jay-Z
9. Ryan Reynolds and Blake Lively
10. John Legend and Chrissy Teigen
11. Prince William and Kate Middleton
12. Ellen DeGeneres and Portia de Rossi

7
1. Mickey Mouse
2. Bugs Bunny
3. Spongebob Squarepants
4. Homer Simpson
5. Snoopy
6. Scooby doo
7. Garfield
8. Tom
9. Jerry
10. Winnie the Pooh
11. Betty Boop
12. Pikachu
13. Hello Kitty
14. Dora the Explorer
15. Bart Simpson
16. Donald Duck

8
1. The Seat Kicker
2. The Talker
3. The Snorer
4. The Smelly Passenger
5. The Crying Child
6. The Parent who doesn't control their child
7. The Food or Drink Spiller
8. The Armrest Hog
9. The Deep Recliner
10. The Frequent Bathroomer
11. The Sick Passenger

9
1. "Scarface" Al Capone
2. "The Teflon Don" John Gotti
3. Charles "Lucky" Luciano
4. Meyer Lansky
5. Frank Costello
6. Benjamin "Bugsy" Siegel
7. Dutch Schultz
8. J.J. "Whitey" Bulger
9. "Big Tuna" Tony Accardo
10. Carlo Gambino
11. John Dillinger
12. Mickey Cohen.

10
1. Gordon Ramsey
2. Jamie Oliver
3. Anthony Bourdain
4. Nigella Lawson
5. Bobby Flay
6. Ina Garten
7. Alton Brown
8. Rachel Ray
9. Guy Fieri
10. Padma Lakshmi
11. Heston Blumental
12. Ree Drummond

Performing Arts 7♥

A	Choose a Question

2	In terms of dancers as of 2019, the 17 largest ballet companies called 15 cities of the world home. Name any of the cities that these largest ballet companies are situated.

3	From 2020 to 2023, 14 of the 15 cities that hosted the most Opera performances were in Europe, all of them with more than 200 per year. Name any of these 15 cities.

4	New York Theater released a list of the best 50 plays of the past 100 years in 2013. 17 Playwrights wrote the top 20 shows. Name any of these playwrights.

5	The Book of Mormon is currently #13 on the list of longest running Broadway shows with about 4,400 performances. Name any of the 12 Musicals that have run longer than The Book of Mormon

6	The Musical Cats has over 30 cat-characters but only 12 of them are important enough to have introductory songs about them. Name these 12 Cats of Cats

7	W.S. Gilbert and Thomas Sullivan collaborated on 14 comic operas between 1871 and 1896. Name any of these operettas

8	According to their Website, the New York Philharmonic has chairs for performers of 9 Woodwind and 5 brass instruments. Name any of these 14 instruments performers blow into at the NY Philharmonic.

9	With apologies to the Schuyler Sisters, in the Musical Hamilton, there were 10 male historical figures portrayed, not including the titular character. Name these 10 Historical Figures.

10	10 Broadway Musicals have won the Pulitzer Prize for Drama. Name any of these 10 Musicals

PERFORMING ARTS 7♥

2
1. Moscow/Bolshoi
2. St Petersburg/Mariinsky
3. Paris/Paris Opera Ballet
4. London/Royal & National
5. Vienna/Staatsballett
6. Milan/Teatro Alla Scala
7. New York/American & New York City
8. Amsterdam/Dutch National
9. Copenhagen/Royal Danish
10. Melbourne/Australian
11. Toronto/National
12. Beijing/National
13. Havana/National
14. Stuttgart/Stuttgart
15. Houston/Houston

3
1. Vienna
2. Moscow
3. London
4. Berlin
5. St Petersburg
6. Munich
7. Paris
8. Hamburg
9. Budapest
10. New York City
11. Dresden
12. Prague
13. Madrid
14. Amsterdam
15. Stockholm

4
1. Arthur Miller
2. Tennessee Williams
3. Edward Albee
4. Eugene O'Neill
5. August Wilson
6. Tony Kushner
7. Samuel Beckett
8. George Bernard Shaw
9. Lorraine Hansberry
10. Luigi Pirandello
11. David Mamet
12. Tracy Letts
13. Sam Shepard
14. John Osbourne
15. Lillian Hellman
16. Tom Stoppard

5
1. The Phantom of the Opera
2. Chicago
3. The Lion King
4. Wicked
5. Cats
6. Les Miserables
7. A Chorus Line
8. Oh! Calcutta!
9. Mamma Mia!
10. Beauty and the Beast
11. Rent
12. Jersey Boys.

6
1. Jennyanydots
2. Rum Tum Tugger
3. Grizabella
4. Bustopher Jones
5. Mungojerrie
6. Rumpleteazer
7. Old Deuteronomy
8. Asparagus
9. Growltiger
10. Skimbleshanks
11. Macavity
12. Mr. Mistoffelees

7
1. Thespis
2. Trial By Jury
3. The Sorcerer
4. HMS Pinafore
5. The Pirates of Penzance
6. Patience
7. Iolanthe
8. The Princess Ida
9. The Mikado
10. Ruddigore
11. The Yeoman of the Guard
12. The Gondoliers
13. Utopia Ltd.
14. The Grand Duke

8
1. Flutes
2. Piccolo
3. Oboes
4. English Horn
5. Clarinet
6. E-Flat Clarinet
7. Bass Clarinet
8. Bassoons
9. Contrabassoon
10. Horns
11. Trumpets
12. Trombones
13. Bass Trombone
14. Tuba

9
1. George Washington
2. King George
3. Marquis De Lafayette
4. Thomas Jefferson
5. Hercules Mulligan
6. James Madison
7. Aaron Burr
8. John Laurens
9. Phillip Hamilton
10. Samuel Seabury

10
1. Of Thee I Sing
2. South Pacific
3. Fiorello!
4. How To Succed in Business Without Really Trying
5. A Chorus Line
6. Sunday in the Park With George
7. Rent
8. Next To Normal
9. Hamilton
10. A Strange Loop

PETS 8♥

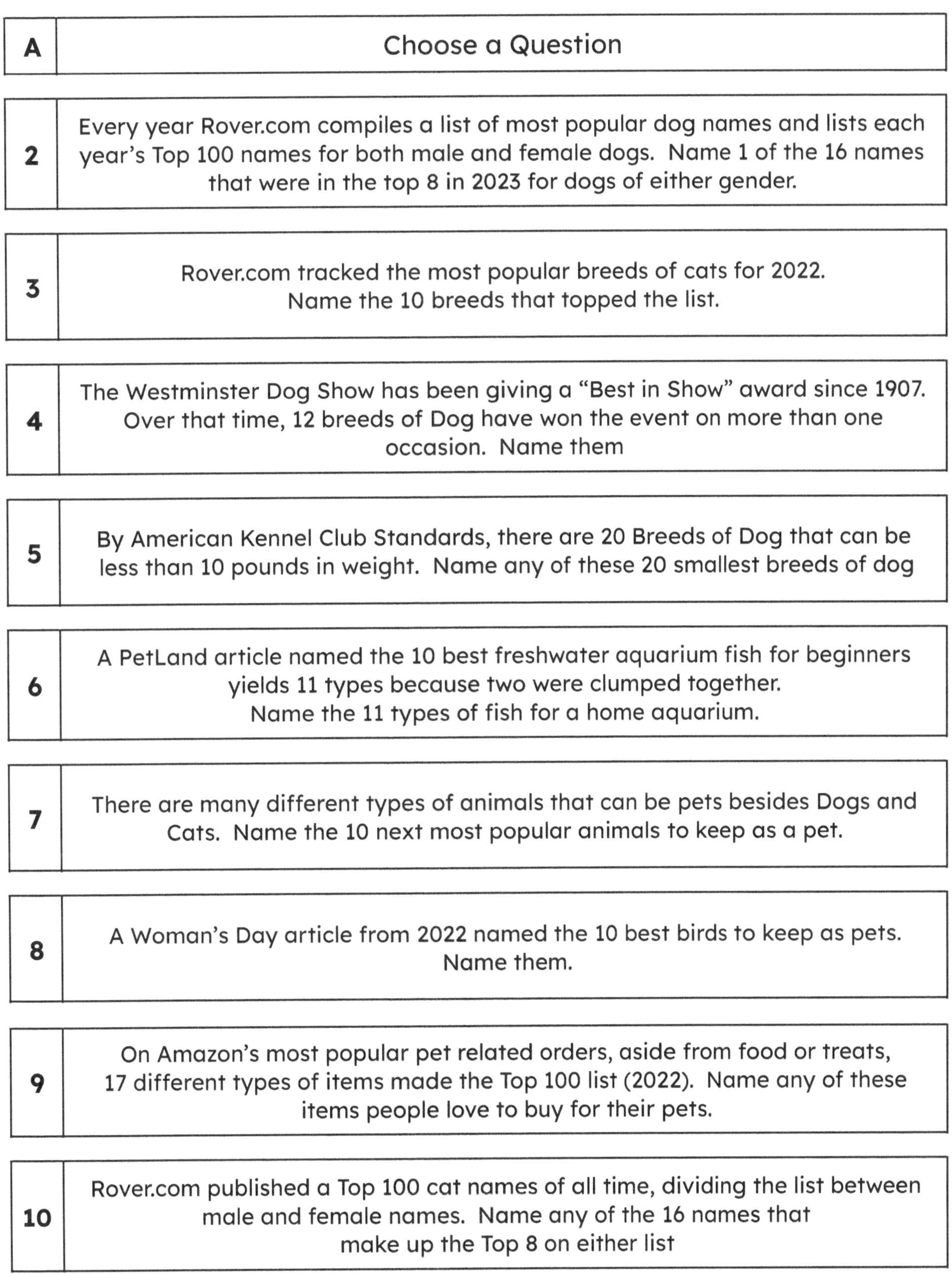

A	Choose a Question
2	Every year Rover.com compiles a list of most popular dog names and lists each year's Top 100 names for both male and female dogs. Name 1 of the 16 names that were in the top 8 in 2023 for dogs of either gender.
3	Rover.com tracked the most popular breeds of cats for 2022. Name the 10 breeds that topped the list.
4	The Westminster Dog Show has been giving a "Best in Show" award since 1907. Over that time, 12 breeds of Dog have won the event on more than one occasion. Name them
5	By American Kennel Club Standards, there are 20 Breeds of Dog that can be less than 10 pounds in weight. Name any of these 20 smallest breeds of dog
6	A PetLand article named the 10 best freshwater aquarium fish for beginners yields 11 types because two were clumped together. Name the 11 types of fish for a home aquarium.
7	There are many different types of animals that can be pets besides Dogs and Cats. Name the 10 next most popular animals to keep as a pet.
8	A Woman's Day article from 2022 named the 10 best birds to keep as pets. Name them.
9	On Amazon's most popular pet related orders, aside from food or treats, 17 different types of items made the Top 100 list (2022). Name any of these items people love to buy for their pets.
10	Rover.com published a Top 100 cat names of all time, dividing the list between male and female names. Name any of the 16 names that make up the Top 8 on either list

PETS 8♥

2
1. Max
2. Charlie
3. Cooper
4. Milo
5. Buddy
6. Rocky
7. Bear
8. Teddy

9. Luna
10. Bella
11. Daisy
12. Lucy
13. Lily
14. Lola
15. Zoe
16. Sadie

3
1. Domestic Shorthair
2. American Shorthair
3. Domestic Longhair
4. Maine Coon
5. Siamese
6. Russian Blue
7. Ragdoll
8. Bengal
9. Bombay
10. Persian

4
1. English Springer Spaniel
2. Standard Poodle
3. Pekingese
4. Airedale Terrier
5. American Cocker Spaniel
6. Boxer
7. Doberman Pinscher
8. Smooth Fox Terrier
9. Sealyham Terrier
10. Miniature Poodle
11. Pointer
12. German Shorthaired Pointer

5
1. Yorkshire Terrier
2. Tiny Fox Terriers
3. Toy Poodles
4. Pomeranians
5. Maltese under
6. Chihuahua under
7. Shih Tzu
8. Rusell Terriers
9. Portuguese Podengo Pequeros
10. Papillons
11. Miniature Pinschers
12. Japanese Chin
13. Italian Greyhound
14. Havanese
15. English Toy Spaniel
16. Coton de Tulear
17. Chinese Crested
18. Brussels Griffon
19. Toy American Eskimo
20. Affenpinschers

6
1. Tetras (Neon)
2. Guppies
3. Mollies
4. Bettas
5. Goldfish
6. Angelfish
7. Barbs (Gold Dwarfs)
8. Rainbowfish
9. Zebrafish
10. Platys
11. Plecos (Algae Eaters

7
1. Fish
2. Birds
3. Rabbits
4. Hamsters
5. Guinea Pigs
6. Ferrets
7. Chickens (Poultry)
8. Horses
9. Turtles
10. Reptiles

8
1. Parakeets (Budgies)
2. Cockatiels
3. Cockatoos
4. Lovebirds
5. Finches
6. Conures
7. Parrotlets
8. Doves
9. Parrots
10. Canaries

9
1. Pee Pads
2. Vitamin Supplements
3. Carpet Cleaner
4. Disposable Cat Litter
5. Chew Toys
6. Pet Crates
7. Pet Beds
8. Pet Toothbrush/paste
9. Odor Elimination Spray
10. Security Cameras
11. Pet Wipes
12. Pet Hair Remover
13. Pet Diapers
14. Shampoo
15. Flea Prevention
16. Feeders
17. Harnesses

10
1. Oliver
2. Milo
3. Leo
4. Charlie
5. Max
6. Loki
7. Simba
8. Jack

9. Luna
10. Lily
11. Bella
12. Lucy
13. Nala
14. Callie
15. Kitty
16. Cleo

PLACES (VS AI) 9♥

A	Choose a Question

2	We asked a Chatbot AI to name the 12 most prestigious (not necessarily best but most impressive) colleges to have a degree from in the United States. Name any of the 12 schools it named.

3	Two AI Chatbots were asked to name the best cities, aside from New York, to use as a setting to write the Great American Novel. Name any of the 16 US Cities the AI recommended

4	We asked an AI Chatbot to name the likely places one's daughter might be going when she says she's going "out." Name any of the 12 answers the Chatbot listed.

5	We asked an AI Chatbot to name the places people commonly go when they wish to "go swimming." Name any of the 10 places named.

6	We asked a Chatbot AI to identify the 12 best kinds of places for a "pleasant bathroom experience" on a long road trip. Name any of these 12 suggested places.

7	An AI Chatbot was asked to name the best brick and mortar stores to register for Wedding Gifts. Name any of the 15 stores it suggested.

8	An AI Chatbot was asked to name some clever places around the house where one could hide money. Name any of the 15 places the AI Chatbot suggested.

9	We asked a Chatbot AI to name some places it would be good to take someone on a first date. Name any of the 13 places suggested.

10	We asked a Chatbot AI to name the best cities in the USA to get a really good slice of pizza. Name any of the 12 cities the AI named.

PLACES (VS AI) 9♥

2
1. Massachusetts Institute of Technology (MIT)
2. Harvard
3. Stanford
4. Yale
5. University of Chicago
6. Princeton
7. Columbia
8. California Institute of Technology (CalTech)
9. University of Pennsylvania
10. Duke
11. Johns Hopkins
12. University of California-Berkeley

3
1. San Francisco, CA
2. New Orleans, LA
3. Chicago, IL
4. Boston, MA
5. Los Angeles, CA
6. Savannah, GA
7. Washington, DC
8. Charleston, SC
9. Seattle, WA
10. Nashville, TN
11. St. Louis, MO
12. Denver, CO
13. Miami, FL
14. Albuquerque, NM
15. Austin, TX
16. Asheville, NC

4
1. Shopping Mall
2. Friend's House
3. Party
4. Movie Theater
5. Concert
6. Sporting Event
7. Beach/pool
8. Downtown
9. Gym
10. Restaurant
11. Park
12. Library/Bookstore

5
1. Swimming Pools
2. Beaches
3. Lakes
4. Rivers
5. Water Parks
6. Hot Springs
7. Quarries
8. Natural Swimming Holes
9. Public Fountains
10. Hotels or Resorts

6
1. Rest Stops
2. Gas Stations
3. Fast Food Restaurants
4. Coffee Shops
5. Supermarkets
6. Restaurants/Diners
7. Hotel/Motels
8. Visitor/Tourist Centers
9. Travel Service Plazas
10. Public Parks
11. Shopping Malls
12. Campgrounds

7
1. Bed Bath and Beyond
2. Macy's
3. Williams Sonoma
4. Crate & Barrel
5. Pottery Barn
6. Target
7. Bloomingdale's
8. Sur La Table
9. Nordstrom
10. Neiman Marcus
11. Anthropologie
12. REI
13. Home Depot
14. Kohl's
15. JCPenney

8
1. Hollowed out Books
2. Artificial Plant
3. Stuffed Animal
4. Tape under Furniture
5. Fake Electrical Outlet
6. Empty Food Container
7. False Bottomed Drawer
8. Picture Frame
9. Toilet Paper Roll
10. Wall Clock
11. Shoes
12. Flashlight
13. Curtain Rod
14. Tissue Box
15. Loose Floorboard

9
1. Coffee Shop/Cafe
2. Botanical Garden
3. Art Museum or Gallery
4. Mini Golf Course
5. Food Truck Park
6. Boardwalk or Pier
7. Picnic in the Park
8. Local Farmers' Market
9. Planetarium
10. Cooking Class
11. Arcade
12. Amusement Park
13. Winery/Brewery Tour

10
1. New York City
2. Chicago
3. New Haven
4. Philadelphia
5. Detroit
6. Providence
7. San Francisco
8. Portland
9. Boston
10. St. Louis
11. Austin, TX
12. Phoenix

QUESTIONS PAIRED 10♥

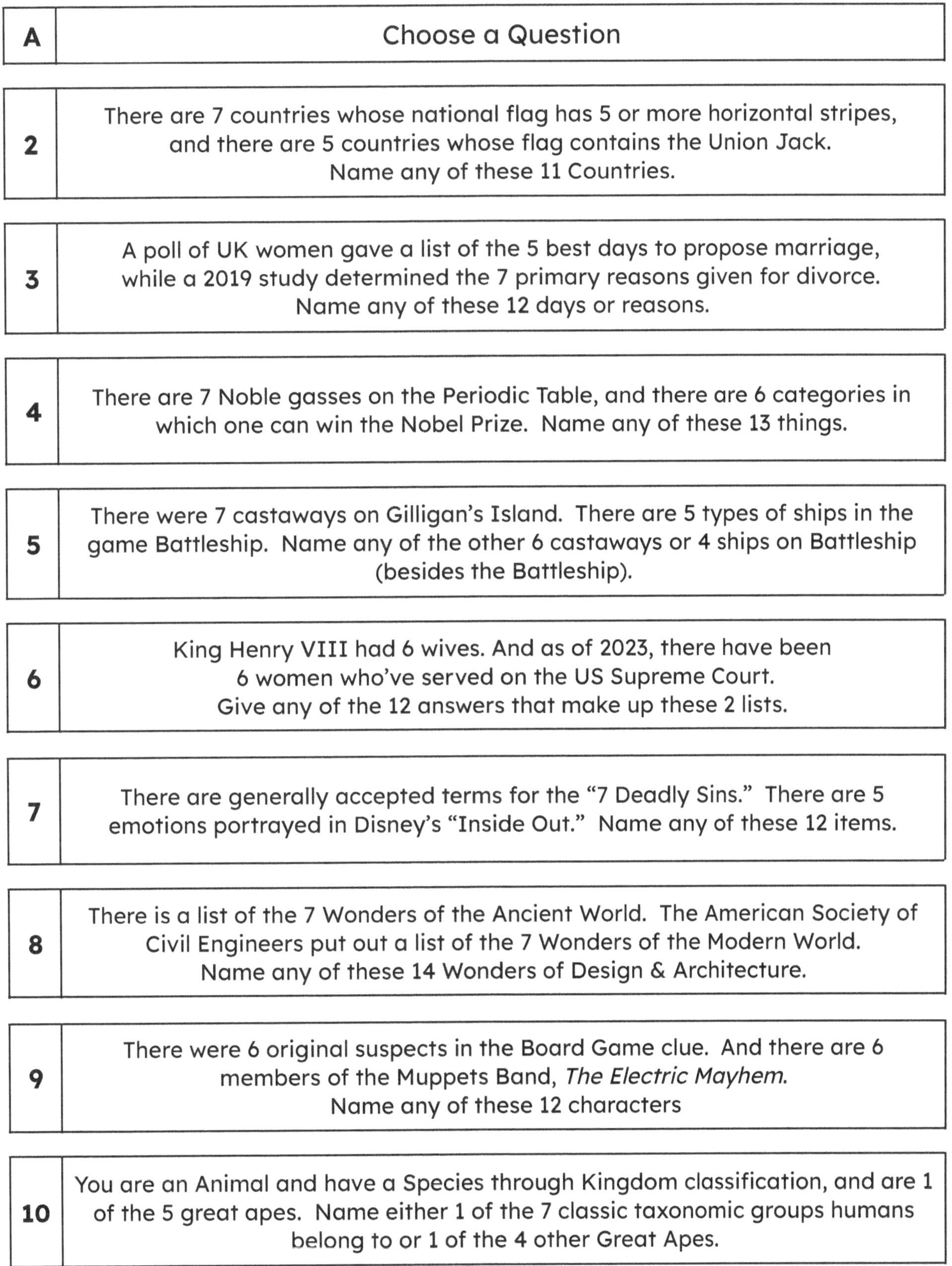

A	Choose a Question
2	There are 7 countries whose national flag has 5 or more horizontal stripes, and there are 5 countries whose flag contains the Union Jack. Name any of these 11 Countries.
3	A poll of UK women gave a list of the 5 best days to propose marriage, while a 2019 study determined the 7 primary reasons given for divorce. Name any of these 12 days or reasons.
4	There are 7 Noble gasses on the Periodic Table, and there are 6 categories in which one can win the Nobel Prize. Name any of these 13 things.
5	There were 7 castaways on Gilligan's Island. There are 5 types of ships in the game Battleship. Name any of the other 6 castaways or 4 ships on Battleship (besides the Battleship).
6	King Henry VIII had 6 wives. And as of 2023, there have been 6 women who've served on the US Supreme Court. Give any of the 12 answers that make up these 2 lists.
7	There are generally accepted terms for the "7 Deadly Sins." There are 5 emotions portrayed in Disney's "Inside Out." Name any of these 12 items.
8	There is a list of the 7 Wonders of the Ancient World. The American Society of Civil Engineers put out a list of the 7 Wonders of the Modern World. Name any of these 14 Wonders of Design & Architecture.
9	There were 6 original suspects in the Board Game clue. And there are 6 members of the Muppets Band, *The Electric Mayhem*. Name any of these 12 characters
10	You are an Animal and have a Species through Kingdom classification, and are 1 of the 5 great apes. Name either 1 of the 7 classic taxonomic groups humans belong to or 1 of the 4 other Great Apes.

QUESTIONS PAIRED 10♥

2
1. Cuba
2. Greece
3. Liberia
4. Malaysia
5. Togo
6. Uruguay
7. USA

8. Australia
9. Fiji
10. New Zealand
11. Tuvalu
12. United Kingdom

3
1. Valentine's Day
2. Day they Met
3. Christmas Eve
4. New Year's Day
5. Christmas Day

6. Infidelity
7. Incompatibility
8. Immaturity
9. Emotional Abuse
10. Finances
11. Unresponsiveness to Needs
12. Drug/Alcohol Abuse

4
1. Helium
2. Argon
3. Krypton
4. Neon
5. Xenon
6. Radon
7. Oganesson

8. Physics
9. Chemistry
10. Medicine (Physiology)
11. Literature
12. Peace
13. Economics

5
1. The Skipper (Jonas Grumby)
2. The Professor (Roy Hinkley)
3. Thurston Howell III
4. Eunice "Lovey" Howell
5. Ginger Grant
6. Mary Ann Summers

7. Carrier
8. Cruiser
9. Submarine
10. Destroyer

6
1. Katherine of Aragon
2. Anne Boleyn
3. Jane Seymour
4. Anne of Cleves
5. Catherine Howard
6. Katherine Parr

7. Sandra Day O'Connor
8. Ruth Bader Ginsberg
9. Elena Kagan
10. Sonia Sotomayor
11. Amy Coney Barrett
12. Kentanji Brown-Jackson

7
1. Pride
2. Greed
3. Wrath
4. Envy
5. Lust
6. Gluttony
7. Sloth

8. Joy
9. Sadness
10. Fear
11. Anger
12. Disgust

8
1. Great Pyramids of Giza
2. Colossus of Rhodes
3. Hanging Gardens of Babylon
4. Lighthouse of Alexandria
5. Mausoleum of Halicarnassus
6. Statue of Zeus at Olympia
7. Temple of Artemis at Ephesus

8. Channel Tunnel
9. CN Tower
10. Empire State Building
11. Golden Gate Bridge
12. Itaipu Dam
13. Delta & Zuiderzee Works
14. Panama Canal

9
1. Miss Scarlett
2. Colonel Mustard
3. Mrs. White
4. Reverend Mr. Green
5. Mrs Peacock
6. Professor Plum

7. Dr. Teeth
8. Floyd Pepper
9. Janice
10. Lips
11. Zoot
12. Animal

10
1. Animalia
2. Chordata
3. Mammalia
4. Primates
5. Hominidae
6. Homo
7. Sapiens

8. Gorilla
9. Chimpanzee
10. Orangutan
11. Bonobo

REALITY TV J♥

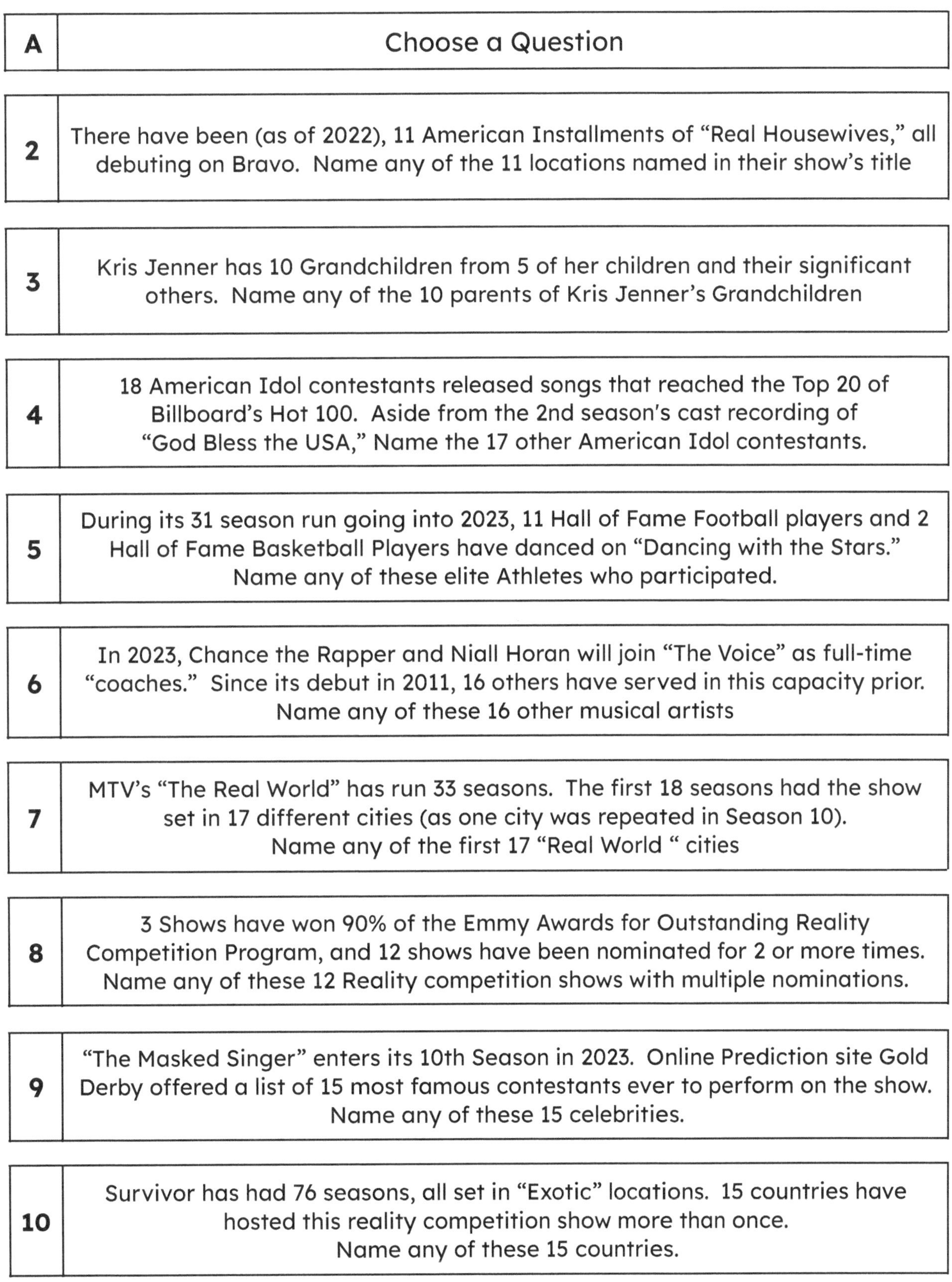

A	Choose a Question
2	There have been (as of 2022), 11 American Installments of "Real Housewives," all debuting on Bravo. Name any of the 11 locations named in their show's title
3	Kris Jenner has 10 Grandchildren from 5 of her children and their significant others. Name any of the 10 parents of Kris Jenner's Grandchildren
4	18 American Idol contestants released songs that reached the Top 20 of Billboard's Hot 100. Aside from the 2nd season's cast recording of "God Bless the USA," Name the 17 other American Idol contestants.
5	During its 31 season run going into 2023, 11 Hall of Fame Football players and 2 Hall of Fame Basketball Players have danced on "Dancing with the Stars." Name any of these elite Athletes who participated.
6	In 2023, Chance the Rapper and Niall Horan will join "The Voice" as full-time "coaches." Since its debut in 2011, 16 others have served in this capacity prior. Name any of these 16 other musical artists
7	MTV's "The Real World" has run 33 seasons. The first 18 seasons had the show set in 17 different cities (as one city was repeated in Season 10). Name any of the first 17 "Real World " cities
8	3 Shows have won 90% of the Emmy Awards for Outstanding Reality Competition Program, and 12 shows have been nominated for 2 or more times. Name any of these 12 Reality competition shows with multiple nominations.
9	"The Masked Singer" enters its 10th Season in 2023. Online Prediction site Gold Derby offered a list of 15 most famous contestants ever to perform on the show. Name any of these 15 celebrities.
10	Survivor has had 76 seasons, all set in "Exotic" locations. 15 countries have hosted this reality competition show more than once. Name any of these 15 countries.

REALITY TV J♥

2
1. Orange County
2. New York City
3. Atlanta
4. New Jersey
5. D.C.
6. Beverly Hills
7. Miami
8. Potomac
9. Dallas
10. Salt Lake City
11. Dubai

3
1. Kortney Kardsahian
2. Scott Disick
3. Kim Kardashian
4. Kanye West
5. Khloe Kardashian
6. Tristan Thompson
7. Rob Kardashian
8. Blac Chyna
9. Kyle Jenner
10. Travis Scott

4
1. Lauren Alaina
2. Adam Lambert
3. Blake Lewis
4. Jordin Sparks
5. Diana DeGarmo
6. Katherine McPhee
7. Kris Allen
8. Scott McCreery
9. Carrie Underwood
10. Phillip Phillips
11. David Cook
12. Bo Bice
13. Ruben Studdard
14. Taylor Hicks
15. Fantasia
16. Kelly Clarkson
17. Clay Aiken

5
1. Jerry Rice
2. Emmitt Smith
3. Jason Taylor
4. Warren Sapp
5. Lawrence Taylor
6. Michael Irvin
7. Kurt Warner
8. Calvin Johnson
9. Terrell Owens
10. Ray Lewis
11. DeMarcus Ware
12. Kareem Abdul Jabbar
13. Clyde Drexler

6
1. Blake Shelton
2. Adam Levine
3. Christina Aguilera
4. CeeLo Green
5. Shakira
6. Usher
7. Gwen Stefani
8. Pharrell Williams
9. Miley Cyrus
10. Alicia Keys
11. Jennifer Hudson
12. Kelly Clarkson
13. John Legend
14. Nick Jonas
15. Ariana Grande
16. Camila Cabello

7
1. New York
2. Los Angeles
3. San Francisco
4. London
5. Miami
6. Boston
7. Seattle
8. Hawaii (Honolulu)
9. New Orleans
10. Chicago
11. Las Vegas
12. Paris
13. San Diego
14. Philadelphia
15. Austin
16. Key West
17. Denver

8
1. The Amazing Race
2. Top Chef
3. Project Runway
4. Dancing with the Stars
5. The Voice
6. American Idol
7. RuPaul's Drag Race
8. Survivor
9. So You Think you Can Dance
10. American Ninja Warrior
11. Nailed It!
12. The Apprentice

9
1. Kermit the Frog (Snail)
2. Dick Van Dyke (Gnome)
3. Rudy Guiliani (Jack-in-the-Box)
4. Gladys Knight (Bee)
5. William Shatner (Knight)
6. Bog Saget (Squiggly Monster)
7. Caitlyn Jenner (Phoenix)
8. Lil Wayne (Robot)
9. LeAnn Rimes (Sun)
10. Drew Carey (Llama)
11. Patti LaBelle (Flower)
12. Busta Rhymes (Dragon)
13. Jewel (Queen of Hearts)
14. Donny Osmond (Peacock)
15. Sarah Palin (Bear)
16. Kristy Alley (Baby Mammoth)

10
1. France
2. Indonesia
3. USA
4. Italy
5. Laos
6. Guatemala
7. Peru
8. Russia
9. Thailand
10. New Zealand
11. Japan
12. India
13. United Kingdom
14. Bolivia
15. Canada

RELIGION Q♥

A	Choose a Question

2	The 266 Popes have adopted a papal name upon Ascension. 13 Names have been used by 6 or more popes. Name these 13 most popular Pope's names.

3	According to Goodreads.com, the 14th Best Holy Book is the I Ching. Name any of the top 13 Holy Books on this list

4	Just missing this list at #14 is Ethiopia, with just under 35 million Muslim residents. Name any of the 13 countries with the most Islamic adherents.

5	It's hard to pin down Abraham Lincoln, Andrew Johnson, or Thomas Jefferson as to faith, but the remaining US Presidents belonged to 12 different church denominations. Name the 12 faiths.

6	Religion is big business in America. There are 14 living Church Pastors that have amassed a net worth of $5 million or more, as of 2022. Name any of the wealthiest U.S. Pastors.

7	About 85% of the World believes in some sort of religion. Putting aside traditional ethnic religions, name any of the 11 largest named faiths by number of adherents

8	There are 27 Books in the New Testament. 15 of those books have a name in the title. Name any of the 10 names from the Titles of New Testament Books.

9	The Gospels and Book of Acts name 13 apostles, due to 1 Replacement. Name any of the 13 Biblical Apostles.

10	The majority of American churchgoers are Protestant. The African Methodist Episcopol Zion Church is the 15th largest with around 1.4 million members. Give the specific name of the 14 largest U.S. Protestant denominations

RELIGION Q♥

2
1. John
2. Benedict
3. Gregory
4. Clement
5. Innocent
6. Leo
7. Pius
8. Boniface
9. Stephen
10. Alexander
11. Urban
12. Paul
13. Adrian

3
1. The Holy Bible
2. The Book of Mormon
3. The Quran
4. The Bhagavad Gita
5. Tao Te Ching
6. The Upanishads
7. The Dhammapada
8. Jesus the Christ: A Study of the Messiah by James Talmadge
9. The Torah
10. The Book of the Law by Aleister Crowley
11. The Analects by Confucius
12. Mahabharata
13. The Egyptian Book of the Dead

4
1. Indonesia
2. Pakistan
3. India
4. Bangladesh
5. Nigeria
6. Egypt
7. Iran
8. Turkey
9. Algeria
10. Sudan
11. Iraq
12. Afghanistan
13. Morocco

5
1. Episcopalian
2. Presbyterian
3. Dutch Reformed
4. Congregationalist
5. Northern Baptist
6. Southern Baptist
7. Methodist
8. Disciples of Christ
9. Churches of Christ
10. Quaker
11. Unitarian
12. Roman Catholic

6
1. Kenneth Copeland
2. Pat Robertson
3. Joel Osteen
4. Benny Hinn
5. Steven Furtick Jr
6. Creflo Dollar
7. Rick Warren
8. Jesse Duplantis
9. T.D. Jakes
10. Franklin Graham
11. Joyce Meyer
12. Paula White
13. Noel Jones
14. John Charles Hagee

7
1. Christianity
2. Islam
3. Hinduism
4. Buddhism
5. Sikhism
6. Spiritism
7. Judaism
8. Baha'i
9. Jainsim
10. Shinto
11. Cao Dai

8
1. Matthew
2. Mark
3. Luke
4. John
5. Timothy
6. Titus
7. Philemon
8. James
9. Peter
10. Jude

9
1. Simon Peter
2. Andrew
3. James, Son of Zebedee
4. John, Son of Zebedee
5. Philip
6. Bartholomew
7. Thomas
8. Matthew/Levi
9. James, Son of Alphaeus
10. Thaddeus
11. Simon the Zealot (of Canaan)
12. Matthias
13. Judas Iscariot

10
1. Southern Baptist
2. United Methodist
3. Church of God in Christ
4. National Baptist
5. Evangelical Lutheran Church
6. National Baptist
7. Assemblies of God
8. Presbyterian
9. African Methodist
10. National Missionary Baptist
11. Lutheran-Missouri Synod
12. Epicscopal
13. Churches of Christ
14. Pentecostal Assemblies of the WOrld
15. African Methodist Episcopol Zion Church

SCIENCES K♥

A	Choose a Question

2	There are many organelle in a plant cell. Omaha Public schools has a coloring page for one. Name the 11 Organelle this public school system believes a 2nd grader should be familiar enough with to include.

3	LiveScience published an article in 2023 detailing 20 "Inventions that changed the world." Name any of these 20 Life-changing Inventions

4	If you were to attend the Massachusetts Institute of Technology, you would have the choice of 13 different Engineering degrees. Name them.

5	If you were to plummet from Space to Earth straight through to the center of the Planet, you would pass through 5 atmospheric layers and 5 major layers of the Earth. Name these 10 layers.

6	How Stuff Works science writers posted a list in 2021 of Laws and Scientific Theories "You should know" Name these 10 scientific principles of which you should be familiar.

7	The NOAA website defines 10 different types of Cloud formations. Name any of them.

8	In 1936, to celebrate the US Patent Office's centennial, they put out a list of the 14 US patented inventions of the previous 100 years that have done the most to "Change Life in America." Name any of these 14 Inventions.

9	According to Astrophysicist Michael Hart's 1992 Update to his book about the 100 most influential persons in history, 12 of the first 25 were scientists or inventors. Name these important scientists in History.

10	Many different Animals are used in Scientific testing. The Humane Society spotlights 11 kinds of animals commonly used on their website. Name any of these 11 types of Animals

Sciences K♥

2
1. Cytoplasm
2. Nucleus
3. Nucleolus
4. Mitochondria
5. Golgi Body
6. Chloroplasts
7. Ribosomes
8. Endoplasmic Reticulum
9. Vacuole
10. Cell Membrane
11. Cell Wall

3
1. Wheel
2. Printing Press
3. Penicillin
4. Compass
5. Light Bulb
6. Telephone
7. Internal Combustion Engine
8. Contraceptives
9. Internet
10. Nails
11. Fire
12. Concrete
13. Magnifying Glass
14. Batteries
15. Marine Chronometer
16. Airplane
17. Refrigerator
18. Nuclear Energy
19. Vaccines
20. X-Rays

4
1. Aerospace
2. Biological
3. Biomedical
4. Chemical
5. Chemical-Biological
6. Civil
7. Computer Science
8. Electrical
9. Environmental
10. Materials Science
11. Mechanical
12. Mechanical and Ocean
13. Nuclear Science

5
1. Exosphere
2. Thermosphere
3. Mesosphere
4. Stratosphere
5. Troposphere
6. Lithosphere (Crust)
7. Asthenosphere
8. Mantle
9. Outer Core
10. Inner Core

6
1. Big Bang Theory
2. Hubble's Law of Cosmic Expansion
3. Kepler's Law of Planetary Motion
4. Universal Law of Gravitation
5. Newton's Laws of Motion
6. Laws of Thermodynamics
7. Archimedes' Buoyancy Principle
8. Evolution and Natural Selection
9. Theory of General Relativity
10. Heisenberg's Uncertainty Principle

7
1. Stratocumulus
2. Cumulus
3. Stratus
4. Cumulonimbus
5. Altocumulus
6. Nimbostratus
7. Altostratus
8. Cirrus
9. Cirrostratus
10. Cirrocumulus

8
1. The Telephone
2. The Electric Telegraph
3. The Electric LIght
4. The Cinema
5. The Gramophone
6. The Commercial Steamboat
7. The Aeroplane
8. Air Brakes for Trains
9. The Linotype Machine
10. The Sewing Machine
11. The Cotton Gin
12. Rubber Vulcanization Process
13. Reaping Machine
14. Aluminum Manufacturing

9
1. Isaac Newton
2. Cai Lun
3. Johannes Gutenberg
4. Albert Einstein
5. Louis Pasteur
6. Galileo Galilei
7. Charles Darwin
8. Nicolaus Copernicus
9. Antoine Lavoisier
10. James Watt
11. Michael Faraday
12. James Clerk Maxwell

10
1. Dogs
2. Monkeys
3. Mice
4. Cats
5. Ferrets
6. Pigs
7. Rabbits
8. Sheep
9. Rats
10. Baboons
11. Horses

SECOND WORDPLAY A♠

A	Choose a Question

2	According to the Free Dictionary, there are 13 words in the English Language that are both 8 letters long and begin with "Free." Name any of these 13 words

3	We asked an AI Chatbot to name the First 15 adjectives that come to mind when it thinks of the word "Friend." Name any of these 15 words.

4	There are 12 words of 9, 10, or 11 letters in length that end in -front. Name any of these 12 words.

5	According to Thesaurus.com, there are 15 close synonyms for the word "Dirty." Name any of these 15 words.

6	There are 15 words in the English language that begin with Q-U-A, not counting plurals. Name any of these 15 words

7	According to the Free Dictionary, there are 13 words with 7, 8, or 9 letters that begin with Love-. Name any of these 13 words

8	According to Dictionary.com, there are 12 English language compound words that end with -print. Name any of these 12 words.

9	Thesaurus.com gives 15 one-word synonyms for the word Intoxicated. Name any of these 15 words.

10	There are 13 compound words, according to the Free dictionary, that are both 7 letters long and end in -bag. Name any of these 13 words

Second Wordplay A♠

2
1. Freehold
2. Freehand
3. Freewill
4. Freeboot
5. Freedmen
6. Freeness
7. Freedman
8. Freeform
9. Freeload
10. Freezing
11. Freeware
12. Freeborn
13. Freebase

3
1. Loyal
2. Supportive
3. Trustworthy
4. Caring
5. Understanding
6. Kind
7. Reliable
8. Fun
9. Generous
10. Compassionate
11. Encouraging
12. Thoughtful
13. Genuine
14. Affectionate
15. Considerate

4
1. Battlefront
2. Storefront
3. Oceanfront
4. Breakfront
5. Waterfront
6. Beachfront
7. Housefront
8. Riverfront
9. Shorefront
10. Shirtfront
11. Forefront
12. Lakefront

5
1. Contaminated
2. Crummy
3. Disheveled
4. Dusty
5. Filthy
6. Greasy
7. Grimy
8. Messy
9. Muddy
10. Murky
11. Nasty
12. Polluted
13. Sloppy
14. Stained
15. Unkempt

6
1. Quake
2. Quart
3. Quash
4. Qualm
5. Quasi
6. Quark
7. Quant
8. Quaff
9. Quaky
10. Quass
11. Quail
12. Quack
13. Quale
14. Quare
15. Quate

7
1. Lovemaker
2. Loveless
3. Lovelorn
4. Lovesome
5. Loveable
6. Lovelily
7. Lovesick
8. Lovevine
9. Lovelock
10. Lovebird
11. Loveseat
12. Lovefest
13. Lovebug

8
1. fingerprint
2. thumbprint
3. voiceprint
4. footprint
5. handprint
6. soleprint
7. blueprint
8. overprint
9. hoofprint
10. newsprint
11. workprint
12. offprint

9
1. Tipsy
2. Blind
3. Bombed
4. Boozed
5. Drunk
6. Inebriated
7. Loaded
8. Looped
9. Muddled
10. Potted
11. Smashed
12. Tanked
13. High
14. Sloppy
15. Tight

10
1. Handbag
2. Mailbag
3. Dirtbag
4. Workbag
5. Nosebag
6. Beanbag
7. Scumbag
8. Fleabag
9. Footbag
10. Sandbag
11. WIndbag
12. Feedbag
13. Postbag

SOCCER 2♠

A	Choose a Question

2	The 2026 World Cup will be hosted jointly by the USA, Canada & Mexico. Name the host country or countries of the 12 previous World Cups

3	In 1982, the NCAA began the Women's College Cup. Through 2022, only 11 schools have won the Championship and 7 other schools have played in the Final game. Name any of these 18 Best Women's College Soccer Programs.

4	The CONCACAF is one of FIFA's regional Governing bodies. 11 teams from CONCACAF have qualified for the World Cup. Name any of the 11 countries.

5	At the 2019 Women's World Cup, MSN.com published a list of the Best US National Women's Soccer team players of all time. Name any soccer player in the top 15.

6	For the 2023-24 season, 10 English Premier league teams play either in Metro London or further South. Name these 10 Southernmost Premier League Football Clubs

7	The Chicago Fire FC as of 2023 plays in Major League Soccer's Eastern Conference. 14 teams in 13 cities are West of Chicago and make up the Western Conference. Name these 13 North American Cities

8	In 2022, the 22nd World Cup was completed. In its history 8 countries have won, and another 5 have made the final match. Name any of the 13 countries whose soccer teams have played in a World Cup Final

9	In 2019, Sports Illustrated put out a list of the greatest Soccer players of all time. AC Milan's Franco Baresi was #16. Name any of the star Soccer players that were listed ahead of him

10	Since the English Premier League began in 1992, 14 teams have accumulated over 200 team wins. Name these 14 teams with the most soccer victories.

Soccer 2♠

2
1. Qatar
2. Russia
3. Brazil
4. South Africa
5. Germany
6. Korea (So)/Japan
7. France
8. USA
9. Italy
10. Mexico
11. Spain
12. Argentina

3
1. North Carolina
2. Florida State
3. Stanford
4. Notre Dame
5. Santa Clara
6. USC
7. Portland
8. UCLA
9. Penn State
10. Florida
11. George Mason
12. BYU
13. West Virginia
14. Duke
15. Connecticut
16. Wisconsin
17. Colorado College
18. Central Florida

4
1. Mexico
2. United States
3. Costa Rica
4. Honduras
5. Canada
6. El Salvador
7. Cuba
8. Haiti
9. Jamaica
10. Trinidad & Tobago
11. Panama

5
1. Mia Hamm
2. Abby Wambach
3. Kristine Lilly
4. Michelle Akers
5. Carli Lloyd
6. Hope Solo
7. Julie Foudy
8. Christine Rampone (Pearce)
9. Alex Morgan
10. Tiffeny Milbrett
11. Brandi Chastain
12. Carin Jennings-Gabarra
13. Brian Scurry
14. Joy Fawcett
15. Megan Rapinoe

6
1. Arsenal
2. Chelsea
3. Tottenham Hotspur
4. Crystal Palace
5. West Ham
6. Fulham
7. Brentford
8. Luton Town
9. Bournemouth
10. Brighton & Hove Albion

7
1. St. Louis
2. Minneapolis
3. Kansas City
4. Houston
5. Dallas
6. Austin
7. Denver
8. Salt Lake City
9. Los Angeles (2 teams)
10. San Jose
11. Portland
12. Seattle
13. Vancouver

8
1. Brazil
2. Germany
3. Italy
4. Argentia
5. France
6. Uruguay
7. England
8. Spain
9. Netherlands
10. Hungary
11. Czechoslovakia
12. Sweden
13. Croatia

9
1. Cristiano Ronaldo
2. Ferenc Puskas
3. Paolo Maldini
4. Gerd Muller
5. Mane Garrincha
6. Alfredo Di Stefano
7. Roberto Baggio
8. Michel Platini
9. Ronaldo
10. Zinedine Zidane
11. Johan Cruyff
12. Franz Beckenbauer
13. Lionel Messi
14. Pele
15. Diego Maradona

10
1. Manchester United
2. Arsenal
3. Chelsea
4. Liverpool
5. Tottenham Hotspur
6. Manchester City
7. Everton
8. Newcastle United
9. Aston Villa
10. West Ham United
11. Southampton
12. Blackburn Rovers
13. Leeds United
14. Leicester City

SOUTH AMERICA 3♠

A	Choose a Question

2	For the 12 countries of South America, there are 13 Capital cities because one country splits this role between 2 cities. Name any of the 13 South American Capitals.

3	With 3 countries on this list, South America accounts for nearly half of all the World's Coffee production. Name any of the 10 top coffee producing countries

4	The Tropic of Capricorn passes through the Andes Mountains about 23.5 degrees South of the Equator. It passes through 10 Countries Worldwide. Name these 10 Nations.

5	Online polling website Ranker.com has asked the question, "What are the most beautiful cities in South America?" Name any of the top 15

6	Colombia leads the world in Cocaine production, but only 2 South American countries are on the list of heaviest Cocaine users. Name the 15 countries where 1.5% of the population or more uses this drug.

7	Just 12 Countries make up mainland South America Name them.

8	2 of the 12 mainland South American countries have a Flag that contains neither vertical or horizontal stripes. Name the 10 countries with stripes on their Flag.

9	Venezuela is one of 12 OPEC member nations, and the only one in the Western Hemisphere. Name the 11 other OPEC nations

10	Stan Getz & Astrud Gilberto's "Girl from Ipanema" was #9 on NPR/Jazz24's 2011 list of the 100 quintessential Jazz songs. Name any of the 14 other Artists that had a song in the top 20

SOUTH AMERICA 3♠

2
1. Buenos Aires, Argentina
2. La Paz, Bolivia
3. Sucre, Bolivia
4. Brasilia. Brazil
5. Santiago, Chile
6. Bogota, Colombia
7. Quito, Ecuador
8. Georgetown, Guyana
9. Asuncion, Paraguay
10. Lima, Peru
11. Paramaribo, Suriname
12. Montevideo, Uruguay
13. Caracas, Venezuela

3
1. Brazil
2. Vietnam
3. Colombia
4. Indonesia
5. Ethiopia
6. Honduras
7. India
8. Uganda
9. Mexico
10. Peru

4
1. Namibia
2. Botswana
3. South Africa
4. Mozambique
5. Madagascar
6. Australia
7. Chile
8. Paraguay
9. Argentina
10. Brazil

5
1. Buenos Aires
2. Cartagena, Colombia
3. San Carlos de Bariloche, Argentina
4. Rio de Janeiro, Brazil
5. Cusco, Peru
6. Santiago, Chile
7. Arequipa, Peru
8. San Martin de Los Andes, Argentina
9. Bogota, Colombia
10. Medellin, Colombia
11. Salvador, Brazil
12. Cordoba, Argentina
13. Lima, Peru
14. Santa Marta, Columbia
15. Quito, Ecuador

6
1. Ireland
2. France
3. Denmark
4. Argentina
5. Uruguay
6. Montenegro
7. Netherlands
8. Spain
9. Scotland
10. Australia
11. USA
12. UK
13. Albania

7
1. Brazil
2. Colombia
3. Argentina
4. Peru
5. Venezuela
6. Chile
7. Ecuador
8. Bolivia
9. Paraguay
10. Uruguay
11. Guyana
12. Suriname

8
1. Argentina
2. Bolivia
3. Chile
4. Colombia
5. Ecuador
6. Paraguay
7. Peru
8. Suriname
9. Uruguay
10. Venezuela

9
1. Algeria
2. Angola
3. Congo
4. Equatorial Guinea
5. Gabon
6. Iran
7. Iraq
8. Kuwait
9. Libya
10. Nigeria
11. United Arab Emirates

10
1. Dave Brubeck
2. Miles Davis
3. Duke Ellington
4. Thelonius Monk
5. John Coltrane
6. Weather Rerport
7. Benny Goodman
8. Billie Holliday
9. Dizzy Gillespie
10. Charles Mingus
11. Oliver Nelson
12. Louis Armstron
13. Herbie Hancock
14. Chet Baker

SPORTS 4♠

A	Choose a Question

2	Founded in 1987, the World Polo Championship has seen 5 National Teams win Gold, as well as another 5 teams take Silver or Bronze. Name these 10 elite (Horse) Polo playing nations.

3	There are only 12 ICC certified Test Cricket nations. One team is multinational, representing 15 Caribbean countries and plays as West Indies (or Windies). Name the other 11 Cricket-Playing Nations

4	In the Big 5 North American Pro Sports leagues (NFL, NBA, MLB, NHL, MLS), there are 15 teams that have a color in their team name. Setting aside the 2 repetitive Cardinal teams, name the other 13.

5	Ice Hockey is an International Game. Going into 2023, 13 countries can boast having 2 or more active NHL players. Name any of these 13 countries

6	Sports Illustrated published a list of the Greatest Athletes of the 20th Century back in 1999. NFL's Jim Brown ranked #16. Name any athlete in the Top 15

7	There are 12 cities that have both an NHL and NBA franchise. San Francisco is excluded due to the location of their Hockey team. Name these 12 Cities.

8	According to Wealthygorilla, there are 15 pro-wrestlers with net worths in excess of $15 million dollars. 2 of them have the last name McMahon. Name any of the other 13 richest pro wrestlers.

9	Soccer (Association Football) is well-known as the sport with the most fans WorldWide. Name the next 10 World's most popular sports.

10	Boxing Hall of Fame Writer Ben Carlson listed his Top 20 Heavyweight fighters of all time, marking Mike Tyson down at #17. Name the 16 men he ranked better than Mike Tyson

Sports 4♠

2
1. Argentina
2. Brazil
3. Chile
4. USA
5. Spain
6. England
7. Mexico
8. Australia
9. Italy
10. Uruguay

3
1. Australia
2. England
3. South Africa
4. New Zealand
5. India
6. Pakistan
7. Sri Lanka
8. Zimbabwe
9. Bangladesh
10. Ireland
11. Afghanistan

4
1. New York Red Bulls
2. Chicago White Sox
3. Chicago Blackhawks
4. Toronto Blue Jays
5. Boston Red Sox
6. Detroit Red Wings
7. St Louis Blues
8. Vancouver Whitecaps
9. Cincinnati Reds
10. Cleveland Browns
11. Columbus Blue Jackets
12. Vegas Golden Knights
13. Green Bay Packers

5
1. Canada
2. USA
3. Sweden
4. Russia
5. Finland
6. Czech Republic
7. Switzerland
8. Slovakia
9. Germany
10. Denmark
11. Latvia
12. Belarus
13. Austria

6
1. Muhammed Ali
2. Michael Jordan
3. Babe Ruth
4. Wilt Chamberlain
5. Babe Didrikson-Zaharias
6. Wayne Gretzky
7. Rod Laver
8. Carl Lewis
9. Jack Nicklaus
10. Pele
11. Bill Russell
12. Jim Thorpe
13. Ted Williams
14. Hank Aaron
15. Larry Bird

7
1. New York, NY
2. Los Angeles CA
3. Chicago, IL
4. Dallas-Fort Worth TX
5. Washington DC
6. Philadelphia
7. Miami
8. Boston
9. Minneapolis
10. Denver
11. Detroit
12. Toronto

8
1. Dwayne "The Rock" Johnson
2. Triple H
3. John Cena
4. Steve Austin
5. Hulk Hogan
6. Kurt Angle
7. Stacy Kiebler
8. Chris Jericho
9. Mick Foley
10. Shawn Michaels
11. The Undertaker
12. The Big Show
13. Dave Bautista

9
1. Cricket
2. Basketball
3. Hockey
4. Tennis
5. Volleyball
6. Table Tennis
7. Baseball
8. American Football
9. Rugby
10. Golf

10
1. Joe Louis
2. Muhammed Ali
3. Larry Holmes
4. Rocky Marciano
5. George Foreman
6. Joe Frazier
7. Lennox Lewis
8. Evander Holyfield
9. Gene Tunney
10. Sonny Liston
11. Jack Dempsey
12. Ken Norton
13. Riddick Bowe
14. Jersey Joe Walcott
15. Floyd Patterson
16. Vitali Klitschko

SUNDRIES 5♠

A	Choose a Question

2	As of 2023, 10 US Presidents have an airport named after them. 2 of these are limited use general aviation airports. Name any of the 10 Presidents with an airport named for them.

3	According to 2020 numbers, there are 3 US Newspapers with a circulation over a million, 9 over half a million and 15 over 370k. Name any of these 15 most widely read US Newspapers

4	In Mariah Carey's "All I want for Christmas is You," there are 17 common nouns in the lyrics of the song. Name any of these 17 common nouns.

5	There are 15 road signs in the Florida DMV Driver's Handbook that are colored black and white only. Name any of these 15 road regulatory signs.

6	Bubba Blue tells Forrest Gump in the movie everything he knows about shrimp. He names 8 methods of cooking and 13 Shrimp preparations. Name any of the 13 Shrimp dishes mentioned by Buford "Bubba" Blue in Forrest Gump

7	Through his storied career, Mel Brooks directed 11 films. Name any of these 11 movies.

8	There are 12 cities in the world with a population over 1 million and a name that begins with "Saint" (or some form thereof, often in a native language). Name any of the World's 12 most populous Saint-Something cities.

9	A 2020 UK Chef's Guild survey polled for Britain's least favorite vegetable. Pumpkin and Cabbage tied for 16th least liked. Name any of the 15 vegetables people of the United Kingdom dislike more.

10	Everyone uses toothpaste. 10 brands of toothpaste have at least 5 million US consumers, with 2 having over 100 million. Name the 10 most widely used toothpaste brands in the USA.

SUNDRIES 5♠

2
1. John F Kennedy
2. George H.W. Bush
3. Ronald Reagan
4. Gerald Ford
5. Abraham Lincoln
6. Bill Clinton
7. Dwight D Eisenhower
8. Theodore Roosevelt
9. Jimmy Carter
10. Franklin Roosevelt

3
1. USA Today
2. Wall Street Journal
3. New York Times
4. Los Angeles Times
5. New York Post
6. New York Daily News
7. Washington Post
8. Chicago Tribune
9. Houston Chronicle
10. Arizona Republic
11. Dallas Morning News
12. (New York) Newsday
13. San Francisco Chronicle
14. Boston Globe
15. (Newark) Star-Ledger

4
1. presents
2. tree
3. wish
4. stocking
5. fireplace
6. Day
7. baby
8. Snow
9. mistletoe
10. list
11. reindeer
12. lights
13. sound
14. laughter
15. bells
16. sleigh
17. door

5
1. Railroad Crossing
2. End School Zone
3. Emergency Stopping Only
4. Restricted (Diamond) Lane
5. Slower Traffic Keep Right
6. Begin Right Turn
7. Center Turn Lane
8. Turn Lane
9. Left Lane Must Turn Left
10. No Turn on Red
11. Keep Right
12. One Way
13. Speeding Fined Doubled
14. Speed Limit
15. Pass With Care

6
1. Shrimp Kabobs
2. Shrimp Creole
3. Shrimp Gumbo
4. Pineapple Shrimp
5. Lemon Shrimp
6. Coconut Shrimp
7. Pepper Shrimp
8. Shrimp Soup
9. Shrimp Stew
10. Shrimp Salad
11. Shrimp and Potatoes
12. Shrimp Burger
13. Shrimp Sandwich

7
1. Dracula: Dead and Loving it
2. Robin Hood: Men in Tights
3. Life Stinks
4. Spaceballs
5. History of the World: Part 1
6. High Anxiety
7. Silent Movie
8. Young Frankenstein
9. Blazing Saddles
10. The Twelve Chairs
11. The Producers

8
1. São Paulo, Brazil
2. Santiago, Chile
3. Saint Petersburg, Russia
4. Santo Domingo, Dominican Republic
5. San Juan, Puerto Rico
6. Santa Cruz, Bolivia
7. San Antonio, USA
8. San Jose, Costa Rica
9. San Diego, USA
10. San Luis Potosi
11. San Salvador, El Salvador
12. San Miguel De Tucuman, Argentina

9
1. Brussel Sprouts
2. Artichoke
3. Celery
4. Aubergine (Eggplant)
5. Beets
6. Celeriac
7. Butternut Squash
8. Bok Choy
9. Broccoli
10. Yam
11. Fennel
12. Okra
13. Marrow (Zucchini)
14. Button Mushrooms
15. Jerusalem Artichoke.

10
1. Colgate
2. Crest
3. Tom's of Maine
4. Sensodyne
5. Arm & Hammer
6. Aquafresh
7. Aim
8. Close-Up
9. Pepsodent
10. Ultra Brite

SUPERHEROES 6♠

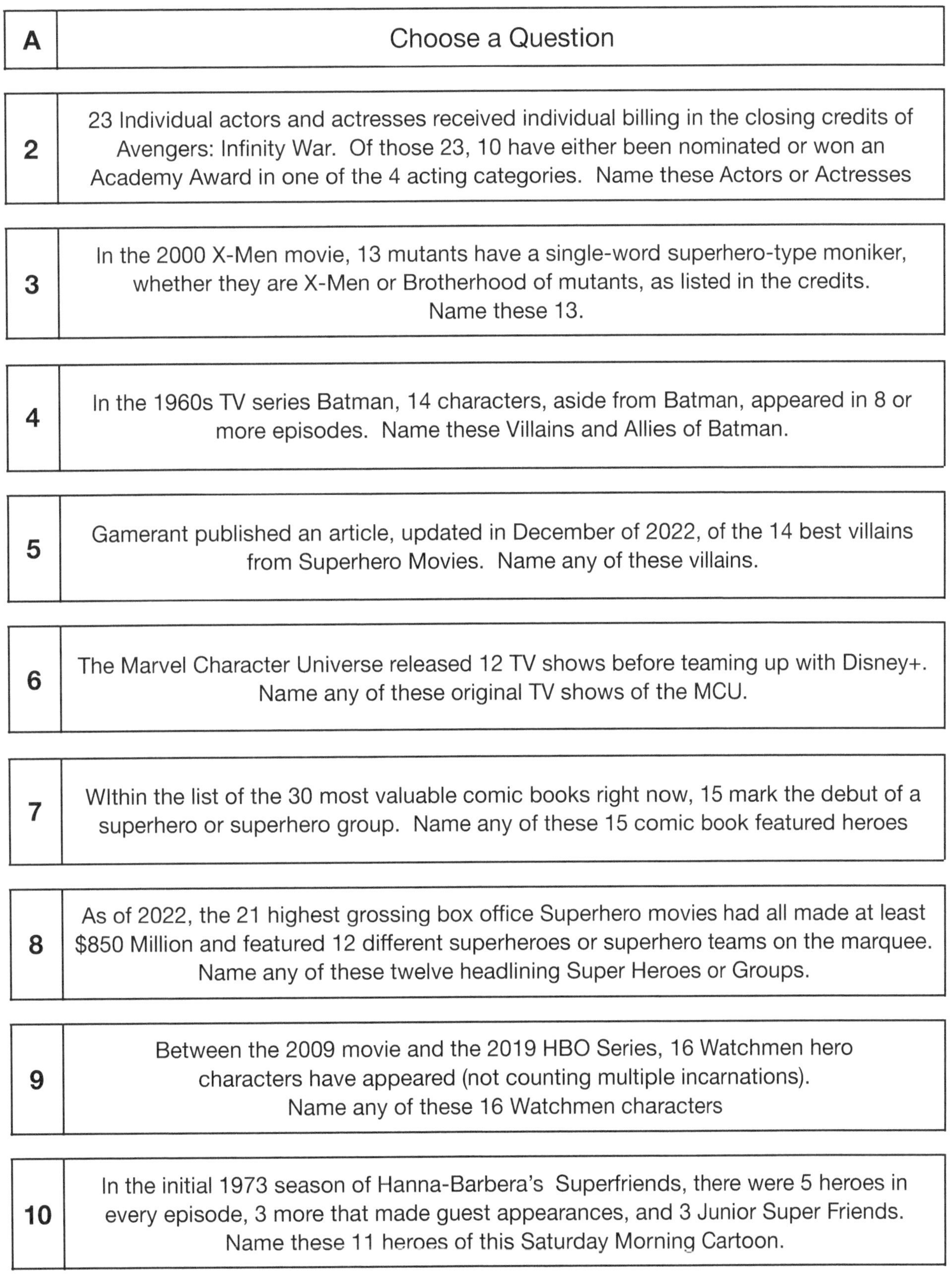

A	Choose a Question
2	23 Individual actors and actresses received individual billing in the closing credits of Avengers: Infinity War. Of those 23, 10 have either been nominated or won an Academy Award in one of the 4 acting categories. Name these Actors or Actresses
3	In the 2000 X-Men movie, 13 mutants have a single-word superhero-type moniker, whether they are X-Men or Brotherhood of mutants, as listed in the credits. Name these 13.
4	In the 1960s TV series Batman, 14 characters, aside from Batman, appeared in 8 or more episodes. Name these Villains and Allies of Batman.
5	Gamerant published an article, updated in December of 2022, of the 14 best villains from Superhero Movies. Name any of these villains.
6	The Marvel Character Universe released 12 TV shows before teaming up with Disney+. Name any of these original TV shows of the MCU.
7	WIthin the list of the 30 most valuable comic books right now, 15 mark the debut of a superhero or superhero group. Name any of these 15 comic book featured heroes
8	As of 2022, the 21 highest grossing box office Superhero movies had all made at least $850 Million and featured 12 different superheroes or superhero teams on the marquee. Name any of these twelve headlining Super Heroes or Groups.
9	Between the 2009 movie and the 2019 HBO Series, 16 Watchmen hero characters have appeared (not counting multiple incarnations). Name any of these 16 Watchmen characters
10	In the initial 1973 season of Hanna-Barbera's Superfriends, there were 5 heroes in every episode, 3 more that made guest appearances, and 3 Junior Super Friends. Name these 11 heroes of this Saturday Morning Cartoon.

SUPERHEROES 6♠

2
1. Robert Downey Jr
2. Don Cheadle
3. Benedict Cumberbatch
4. Chadwick Boseman
5. Bradley Cooper
6. Scarlett Johansson
7. Gwynneth Paltrow
8. Mark Ruffalo
9. Benecio Del Toro
10. Josh Brolin

3
1. Wolverine
2. Magneto
3. Cyclops
4. Storm
5. Rogue
6. Sabretooth
7. Toad
8. Mystique
9. Shadowcat
10. Iceman
11. Jubilee
12. Pyro
13. Cerebro

4
1. Robin
2. Alfred
3. Commissioner Gordon
4. Chief O'Hara
5. Aunt Harriet
6. Batgirl
7. The Joker
8. The Penguin
9. The Catwoman
10. Mayor Linseed
11. Sgt O'Leary
12. Warden Crichton
13. The Riddler
14. King Tut

5
1. The Joker (Dark Night)
2. Mr. Glass (Unbreakable)
3. Magneto (X-men)
4. Ultron (Avengers: Age of Ultron)
5. Killmonger (Black Panther)
6. The Penguin (Batman Returns)
7. Electro (Amazing Spiderman 2)
8. Ozymandia (The Watchmen)
9. Thanos (Avengers: Infinity War)
10. Firefist (Deadpool 2)
11. Amanda Waller (Suicide Squad)
12. Red Mist (Kick Ass)
13. Mystique (X-men First Class)
14. King Pine (Spiderman into the Spiderverse)

6
1. Agents of S.H.I.E.L.D
2. Agent Carter
3. Inhumans
4. Daredevil
5. Jessica Jones
6. Luke Cage
7. Iron Fist
8. The Defenders
9. The Punisher
10. Runaways
11. Cloak & Dagger
12. Helstrom

7
1. The Flash
2. Green Lantern
3. The Avengers
4. Shazam
5. Fantastic Four
6. Incredible Hulk
7. Captain America
8. Iron Man
9. Human Torch
10. Namor the Submariner
11. X-Men
12. Batman
13. Wonder Woman
14. Spiderman
15. Superman

8
1. The Avengers
2. Spiderman
3. Black Panther
4. Iron Man
5. Captain America
6. Aquaman
7. Captain Marvel
8. Batman
9. Doctor Strange
10. Guardians of the Galaxy
11. Venom
12. Thor

9
1. Doctor Manhattan
2. Rorschach
3. The Comedian
4. Hooded Justice
5. Captain Metropolis
6. Silk Spectre
7. Nite Owl
8. Dollar Bill
9. Mothman
10. The Silhouette
11. Ozymandias
12. Looking Glass
13. Sister Night (Manhattan)
14. Lady Manhattan
15. Mimi
16. Marionette

10
1. Superman
2. Batman
3. Robin
4. Aquaman
5. Wonder Woman
6. Marvin White
7. Wendy Harris
8. Wonder Dog
9. Plastic Man
10. The Flash
11. Green Arrow

TELEVISION 7♠

A	Choose a Question

2	ABC's Daytime Talk Show "The View" has run since 1997 and had 24 hosts. Through Season 18 (2015), there were 14 Women who served in this role. Name any of the original 14 hosts of The View

3	Rotten Tomatoes conducted a survey asking "What TV shows defined the 70s?" 14 of the top answers were Prime Time dramas or sitcoms. Name any of these 14 unmistakably 1970s shows.

4	Between *Game of Thrones* & the 1st season of *House of Dragons,* 17 "Houses" are named in HBO's and George R.R. Martin's Westeros world. Name any of these 17 Houses.

5	Kelsey Grammer appeared as Frazier Crane in over 200 episodes of both "Cheers" and "Frazier." 10 other actors appeared in 200 episodes in one of those 2 shows like him. Name either the 10 characters or the actors that portrayed them

6	True Crime is very popular and has dozens of TV shows airing currently. From a poll of True Crime watchers, Name the 12 kinds of Crime they are most likely to want to watch.

7	Debuting in 1968, 60 Minutes didn't have its first female host or correspondent until 1981. Since then 17 women have filled these roles with the show. Name any of these female news people.

8	Glee ran from 2009-2015 as a show centered around a Glee Club. 13 actors or actresses portrayed Glee Club members in 70 or more of the 121 episodes. Give the first name or nickname of any of the 13 characters

9	Watchmojo put out a list of the top 10 most memorable TV Lawyers. With a tie for third, and 5 honorable mentions, the list included 16 characters. Name any of these memorable TV Lawyers

10	Wayne Brady was tied with Dan Rather & Jeff Foxworthy at #16 in a YouGov Poll to find out TV's Most Popular contemporary personalities. Name any of the 16 TV Personalities seen more favorably.

TELEVISION 7♠

2
1. Meredith Viera
2. Star Jones
3. Debbie Matenopoulos
4. Barbara Walters
5. Joy Behar
6. Lisa Ling
7. Elizabeth Hasselbeck
8. Rosie O'Donnell
9. Whoopie Goldberg
10. Sherri Shepherd
11. Jenny McCarthy
12. Nicolle Wallace
13. Rosie Perez
14. Raven-Symone.

3
1. MASH
2. Happy Days
3. All In the Family
4. Charlie's Angels
5. The Brady Bunch
6. The Mary Tyler Moore Show
7. Mork & Mindy
8. Laverne & Shirley
9. Little House on the Prairie
10. The Jeffersons
11. Colombo
12. Taxi
13. The Six Million Dollar Man
14. Sanford and Son

4
1. Targaryen
2. Lannister
3. Stark
4. Martell
5. Tyrell
6. Baratheon
7. Bolton
8. Greyjoy
9. Arryn
10. Tully
11. Frey
12. Cole
13. Westerling
14. Strong
15. Beesbury
16. Velaryon
17. Hightower

5
1. Sam Malone (Ted Danson)
2. Rhea Perlman (Carla Tortelli)
3. John Ratzenberger (Cliff Claven)
4. George Wendt (Norm Peterson)
5. Kelsey Grammer (Dr. Frasier Crane)
6. Woody Harrelson (Woody Boyd)
7. Jane Leeves (Daphne Moon)
8. David Hyde Pierce (Dr. Niles
9. Crane)
10. Peri Gilpin (Roz Doyle)
11. John Mahoney (Martin Crane)

6
1. Murder
2. Serial Killing
3. Kidnapping
4. Sexual Assault
5. Domestic Abuse
6. Corruption
7. Drug Trafficking
8. Robbery
9. Organized Crime
10. Fraud
11. Financial Crime
12. Hacking

7
1. Lesley Stahl
2. Cecilia Vega
3. Norah O'Donnell
4. Sharyn Alfonsi
5. Diane Sawyer
6. Meredith Viera
7. Christiane Amanpour
8. Lara Logan
9. Marlene Sanders
10. Connie Chung
11. Paula Zahn
12. Carol Marin
13. Vicki Mabry
14. Katie Couric
15. Alison Stewart
16. Clarissa Ward
17. Oprah Winfrey

8
1. Kurt (Chris Colfer)
2. Rachel (Lea Michelle)
3. Tina (Jenna Ushkowitz)
4. Artie (Kevin McHale)
5. Santana (Naya Rivera)
6. Tina (Jenna Ushkowitz)
7. Mercedes (Amber Riley)
8. "Puck" or Noah (Mark Sailin)
9. Brittany S Pierce (Heather Morris)
10. Sam Evans (Chord Overstreet)
11. Mike (Harry Shum Jr)
12. Finn (Cory Monteith)
13. Quinn (Dianna Agron)

9
1. Jeffrey Winger (Community)
2. Patty Hewes (Damages)
3. Maury Levy (The Wire)
4. Oliver Babish (The West Wing)
5. Sandy Cohen (The O.C)
6. Ted Buckland (Scrubs)
7. Lionel Hutz (Simpsons)
8. Jack McCoy (Law & Order)
9. Ally McBeal (Ally McBeal)
10. Jackie Chiles (Seinfeld)
11. Dan Fielding (Night Court)
12. Saul Goodman (Breaking Bad)
13. Alan Shore (Boston Legal)
14. Denny Crane (Boston Legal)
15. Ben Matlock (Matlock)
16. Perry Mason (Perry Mason)

10
1. Alex Trebek
2. Bob Barker
3. Steve Harvey
4. Jay Leno
5. Vanna White
6. Drew Carey
7. Barbara Walters
8. Bill Nye
9. Cindy Crawford
10. Jimmy Fallon
11. Sinbad
12. Gordon Ramsey
13. Pat Sajak
14. David Letterman
15. Rachael Ray

r

THE INTERNET 8♠

A	Choose a Question

2	In terms of web sales, Amazon is the clear #1. Costco finishes 2023 in the #15 position Name any of the other 13 of the 15 top Online Retailers in terms of Sales Volume

3	For 2022, the most googled single word was "Facebook." Name the next 12 most googled words (Adult Site related words excluded).

4	.US never caught on like other nation's Top Level Domains with 6 of the top 10 most used TLDs worldwide being country specific. Name any of the 10 Top Level Domains

5	In November of 2023, just as Twitter was taken over by new management, the #15 most followed account was Twitter itself. Name the 14 accounts with more followers on Twitter than Twitter at that time

6	The most used search engine has 92% of the market share. #10 on this list has about 0.05%. Name the Top 10 most used search engines Worldwide.

7	14 Countries have 90% or more of their population with Internet access as of 2021. Small countries with populations of 5 Million or less are excluded. Name these 14 countries

8	20 Musical artists or acts account for more than half of Youtube's most viewed videos of all time (with over 3 Billion views, as of June 2023). Name any of these Artists

9	As of 2023, 6 of the top social media platforms, in terms of active users, were principally used in China (WeChat, Douyin, QQ,Weibo, Kuaishou, Qzone). Aside from these, Name the Top 10 social media platforms

10	Travel websites include information on places to stay and methods of travel. 5 of the top 20 most visited travel sites aren't in English. Name any of the top 15 most visited English Language (DEC 22) travel websites.

THE INTERNET 8♠

2
1. Ebay
2. Kroger
3. Apple
4. Etsy
5. Walmart
6. Ikea
7. Shop BBC
8. The Home Depot
9. Best Buy
10. Infobae
11. Dell
12. HP
13. Target

3
1. Youtube
2. Amazon
3. Weather
4. Walmart
5. Google
6. Wordle
7. Gmail
8. Target
9. Yahoo
10. Costco
11. Starbucks
12. Translate

4
1. .com
2. .org
3. .ru
4. .net
5. .uk
6. .au
7. .in
8. .de
9. .ir
10. .c

5
1. Barack Obama
2. Elon Musk
3. Justin Bieber
4. Katy Perry
5. Rihanna
6. Cristiano Ronaldo
7. Taylor Swift
8. Lady Gaga
9. Narendra Modi
10. YouTube
11. Ellen DeGeneres
12. Kim Kardashian
13. Nasa
14. Selena Gomez

6
1. Google
2. Bing
3. Yahoo
4. Baidu
5. Yandex
6. DuckDuckGo
7. Ask (Formerly Ask Jeeves)
8. Ecosia
9. AOL.com
10. Internet Archive

7
1. UK
2. So. Korea
3. UAE
4. Norway
5. Japan
6. Germany
7. France
8. Denmark
9. Taiwan
10. Switzerland
11. Sweden
12. United States
13. Netherlands
14. Poland

8
1. Luis Fonsi
2. Ed Sheeran
3. Wiz Khalifa
4. Mark Ronson
5. Psy
6. El Chombo
7. Maroon 5
8. Katy Perry
9. OneRepublic
10. Justin Bieber
11. Shakira
12. Allan Walker
13. Passenger
14. Enrique Iglesias
15. Major Lazer
16. Taylor Swift
17. J Balvin & Wily WIlliam
18. Adele
19. Charlie Puth
20. Chainsmokers

9
1. Facebook
2. YouTube
3. What'sApp
4. Instagram
5. TikTok
6. Facebook Messenger
7. Snapchat
8. Telegram
9. Pinterest
10. Twitter

10
1. Booking.com
2. Tripadvisor.com
3. AmericanExpress
4. Agoda.com
5. ryan air
6. air bnb
7. Expedia
8. Flightaware
9. Flightradar24
10. Skyscanner
11. American Airlines
12. Marriott
13. MakemyTrip
14. TheTrainline
15. Hotels.com

THE WORLD 9♠

A	Choose a Question
2	According to Bloomberg at the end of 2022, the 12 richest people in the world were worth between 80 and 200 Billion dollars. Name any of these 12 Billionaires.
3	There are 11 freshwater lakes in the world that are over 20,000 square kilometers by area. Name the 11 largest freshwater lakes of the world
4	There are 18 Islands on Earth that are 100,000 Square Kilometers or larger in area. Name any of the 18 largest Islands in the world.
5	Over 6.8 Million have died from COVID worldwide. 11 Countries have had a death toll of greater than 150,000. Name any of these 11 countries.
6	China and India have populations over a billion. 13 other countries have populations over 100 million. Name these 13 other countries.
7	The English names of the Countries of the World have 7 Nations whose last letter is D, as well as 7 more that end in Y. Name the 14 countries of the world that end in either D or Y
8	According to a 2019 report by the OECD, 11 countries have a population where 50% or more of their populace have college degrees. Name the 11 most educated countries in the world
9	The Kyzylkum Desert of Central Asia is the 16th largest desert in the world measuring approximately 300,000 square kilometers. Name the World's 15 Largest Deserts
10	The Rouen Cathedral in France was the world's tallest building from 1876-1880. Since then 10 buildings have been said to be the World's Tallest Building. Name any of these 10 Architectural feats

THE WORLD 9♠

2
1. Bernard Arnault
2. Elon Musk
3. Jeff Bezos
4. Bill Gates
5. Warren Buffett
6. Larry Ellison
7. Steve Balmer
8. Larry Page
9. Carlos Slim
10. Sergey Brin
11. Mukesh Ambani
12. Francoise Bettencourt Meyers

3
1. Lake Superior
2. Lake Victoria
3. Lake Huron
4. Lake Michigan
5. Lake Tanganyika
6. Lake Baikal
7. Great Bear Lake
8. Lake Malawi
9. Great Slave Lake
10. Lake Erie
11. Lake WInnipeg

4
1. Greenland
2. New Guinea
3. Borneo
4. Madagascar
5. Baffin Island
6. Sumatra
7. Honshu
8. Victoria Island
9. Great Britain
10. Ellesmere Island
11. Sulawesi
12. South Island((Te Waipounamu)
13. Java
14. North Island (Te Ika-a-Maui)
15. Luzon
16. Newfoundland
17. Cuba
18. Iceland

5
1. USA
2. Brazil
3. India
4. Russia
5. Mexico
6. Peru
7. UK
8. Italy
9. Germany
10. France
11. Indonesia

6
1. United States
2. Indonesia
3. Pakistan
4. Nigeria
5. Brazil
6. Bangladesh
7. Russia
8. Mexico
9. Japan
10. Philippines
11. Ethiopia
12. Egypt
13. Vietnam

7
1. Hungary
2. Germany
3. Italy
4. Norway
5. Paraguay
6. Turkey
7. Uruguay
8. Finland
9. Iceland
10. Ireland
11. New Zealand
12. Poland
13. Switzerland
14. Thailand

8
1. South Korea
2. Canada
3. Russia
4. Japan
5. Ireland
6. Lithuania
7. Luxembourg
8. Switzerland
9. Austria
10. United Kingdom
11. United States

9
1. Antarctic
2. Arctic
3. Sahara
4. Great Australian
5. Arabian
6. Gobi
7. Kalahari
8. Patagonian
9. Syrian
10. Great Basin
11. Chihuahuan
12. Karakum
13. Great Victoria
14. Colorado Plateau
15. Sonoran

10
1. Cologne Cathedral
2. Washington Monument
3. Eiffel Tower
4. Chrysler Building
5. Empire State Building
6. World Trade Center
7. Sears Tower
8. Petronas Tower
9. Taipei 101
10. Burj Khalifa.

THINGS (VS A.I.) 10♠

A	Choose a Question

2	We asked an AI Chatbot, at a typical comic con, what TV Shows or Movies do people most commonly dress like. Name any of these 12 shows or franchises.

3	An AI Chatbot was asked to name the toppings needed to have a truly excellent sundae bar at a party. Aside from sauces, it named 14 items. Name them.

4	We asked a Chatbot AI to name the most popular types of salad dressings ordered in restaurants. Name any of the 10 Salad Dressing the AI indicated.

5	We asked an AI Chatbot to name the most popular Chinese dishes Americans order for takeout. Name any of the 13 dishes the AI named

6	A Chatbot AI was asked to name the most common reasons given when a person calls in sick to work. Name any of the 13 conditions the AI listed.

7	We asked a Chatbot AI, to name some of the best toppings for a hamburger, aside from the very traditional like Ketchup or Cheese. Name any of the 12 Hamburger toppings suggestion the AI named

8	We asked an AI Chatbot to name the things women look for the most in a man. Name the 12 things the AI named.

9	An AI Chatbot was asked to name the musical instruments one should learn if one wanted to maximize one's chance to make it in a Rock and Roll Band. Name any of the 12 instruments the AI Named.

10	A Chat AI was asked to name the best tasting breakfast cereals, without regard for nutrition. Name any of the 12 brands of Cereals the AI named.

Things (vs A.I.) 10♠

2
1. Marvel Cinematic Universe
2. DC Extended Universe
3. Star Wars
4. Game of Thrones
5. Strangers Things
6. The Walking Dead
7. Harry Potter
8. The Witcher
9. Doctor Who
10. Star Trek
11. Rick & Morty
12. Anime-Inspired shows

3
1. Whipped Cream
2. Chopped Nuts
3. Sprinkles
4. Crushed Oreos
5. Fresh Berries
6. Sliced Bananas
7. Mini Marshmallows
8. Shredded coconut
9. Chocolate Chips
10. Gummi Bears
11. Cookie Dough Pieces
12. Brownie Chunks
13. Cherries
14. Diced Pineapple

4
1. Ranch
2. Italian
3. Caesar
4. Balsamic Vinaigrette
5. Blue Cheese
6. Thousand Island
7. Honey Mustard
8. Greek
9. French
10. Oil & Vinegar

5
1. General Tso's Chicken
2. Kung Pao Chicken
3. Sweet & Sour Chicken
4. Orange Chicken
5. Egg Rolls
6. Fried Rice
7. Chow Mein
8. Mongolian Beef
9. Beef & Broccoli
10. Lo Mein
11. Szechuan Shrimp
12. Ma Po Tofu
13. Wonton Soup

6
1. Flu
2. Gastrointestinal Issues
3. Cold
4. Child's Illness
5. Food Poisoning
6. Migraine/Headache
7. Fever
8. Toothache/Lost Filling
9. Back Pain
10. Pink Eye
11. Allergic Reactions
12. Sprains/Strains
13. Skin Rashes

7
1. Bacon
2. Fried Egg
3. Avocado
4. Jalapenos
5. Grilled Onions
6. Mushrooms
7. Blue Cheese
8. Guacamole
9. BBQ sauce
10. Cole Slaw
11. Pineapple
12. Sri Racha

8
1. Sense of humor
2. Kindness and empathy
3. Confidence
4. Honesty and integrity
5. Emotional intelligence
6. Similar interests and values
7. Ambition and drive
8. Good communication skills
9. Physical attraction
10. Respectfulness
11. Trustworthiness
12. Being a good listener.

9
1. Guitar
2. Bass
3. Drums
4. Keyboard/Piano
5. Saxophone
6. Harmonica
7. Violin/Fiddle
8. Trumpet
9. Trombone
10. Congas/Bongos
11. Vocals
12. Synthesizer

10
1. Cinnamon Toast Crunch
2. Frosted Flakes
3. Cap'n Crunch
4. Froot Loops
5. Reese's Puffs
6. Lucky Charms
7. Cocoa Puffs
8. Apple Jacks
9. Honey Nut Cheerios
10. Fruity Pebbles
11. Trix
12. Golden Grahams

Travel J♠

A	Choose a Question

2	In the Tropical paradise of the Caribbean, there are 13 fully independent Island nations. Name them

3	The Fontainebleau will open in 2023 and become number 7 on this list, but currently there are 15 Las Vegas hotel/casinos with 3,000 rooms or more. Name these largest Las Vegas hotels.

4	There are 63 US National Parks, 10 of which are the most visited according to Parks Services with over 3.1 million visitors in 2021. Name them.

5	The most recent Gallup poll of Americans (2006) asking where they would go on their dream vacation yielded 12 destinations receiving at least 2% of the vote. Name them. (Hint: the Answer can be a country, US State, or Continent)

6	Based on Pre-Pandemic Numbers (2019), 12 European cities had 6 million or more international visitors. Name these most traveled to European Cities

7	Of the 100 busiest Cruise passenger ports in the world, the Florida Port of Palm Beach ranks 65th, making it the 12th busiest US Cruise Port. Name the 11 busier Cruise ports in the USA

8	12 of the 17 busiest Airports in the world are located in North American Cities, all servicing over 35 million passengers in 2021. Name the cities these airports are associated with.

9	The State of Washington has 157 miles of Ocean shoreline, 11 states have less beachfront than Washington. Name the 11 States with a shoreline, but the least beachfront.

10	Not all of the 10 most popular Cruise destinations are in the Caribbean, with 2 being in the Pacific. Name the 10 places Americans most often choose as a Cruise Destination

Travel J♠

2
1. Cuba
2. Haiti
3. Dominican Republic
4. Jamaica
5. Trinidad & Tobago
6. Bahamas
7. Barbados
8. St. Lucia
9. Grenada
10. St. Vincent and the Grenadines
11. Antigua & Barbuda
12. Dominica
13. St. Kitts & Nevis

3
1. MGM Grand
2. Aria (City Center)
3. Luxor
4. The Venetian
5. Excalibur
6. Bellagio
7. Circus Circus
8. Flamingo
9. Resorts World (Frmly Stardust)
10. Caeser's Palace
11. Mandalay Bay
12. The Palazzo
13. The Mirage
14. Cosmopolitan
15. ParkMGM

4
1. Great Smoky Mountains
2. Zion
3. Chesapeake & Ohio Canal Historic
4. Yellowstone
5. Grand Canyon
6. Rocky Mountain
7. Acadia
8. Grand Teton
9. Yosemite
10. Indiana Dunes

5
1. Hawaii
2. Europe
3. Australia
4. Italy
5. Alaska
6. California
7. Florida
8. Greece
9. London/England
10. Ireland
11. Fiji
12. Bahamas

6
1. London, UK
2. Paris, France
3. Istanbul, Turkey
4. Antalya, Turkey
5. Rome, Italy
6. Prague, Czechia
7. Amsterdam, Netherlands
8. Barcelona, Spain
9. Vienna, Austria
10. Milan, Italy
11. Athens, Greece
12. Berlin, Germany

7
1. Miami
2. Canaveral
3. Everglades (Ft. Lauderdale)
4. Galveston
5. New York and New Jersey
6. New Orleans
7. Juneau
8. Tampa
9. Seattle
10. Ketchikan (AK)
11. Los Angeles

8
1. Atlanta
2. Dallas-Ft Worth
3. Denver
4. Chicago O'Hare
5. Los Angeles
6. Charlotte
7. Orlando
8. Las Vegas (Harry Reid)
9. Phoenix
10. Miami
11. Seattle
12. Mexico City

9
1. New Hampshire
2. Delaware
3. Maryland
4. Rhode Island
5. Mississippi
6. Alabama
7. Connecticut
8. Georgia
9. Virginia
10. New York
11. New Jersey

10
1. Nassau, Bahamas
2. Cozumel, Mexico
3. St. Thomas, US Virgin Islands
4. St Maarten/Martin
5. San Juan, Puerto Rico
6. Glacier Bay National Park, Alaska
7. Key West, Florida
8. Cayman Islands
9. Honolulu, Oahu, Hawaii
10. Grand Turk, Turks and Caicos

The United States Q♠

A	Choose a Question

2	New York and Chicago are the 1st and 3rd most populous US cities. Only 11 other cities East of the Mississippi River have 600,000 or more people. Name these 11 cities of the Eastern United States

3	In 27 U.S. States, the Death Penalty is still legal. However, only 11 states have put a criminal to death in the past 10 years (2013-2023) Name the 11 states with recent executions.

4	There are 12 US states that share a land border with exactly 4 other states. Name any of these 12 states.

5	In 2020, due to COVID, Museum attendance was down about 80% nationwide. The 22 most visited museums were situated in 11 U.S. Cities. Name any of these 11 Cities

6	According to a 2020 study, 13 U.S. States have between 14-20% of their population living below the poverty line. Name any of these 13 poorest states.

7	Because of a tie for #10, US News Top 10 Best US Colleges lists 11 Universities. Name any of the 11 best colleges in the United States

8	The Great Mississippi River runs through or borders 10 US States. Name these 10 states.

9	In the past 50 years (1973-2023) 10 different women have topped Gallup's Poll of America's most admired women. Name them.

10	The 16 largest cities within 100 miles of the Gulf of Mexico range in population from just over 150 thousand to over 2 million. Name any of the 16 largest cities within 100 miles of the Gulf of Mexico.

The United States Q♠

2
1. Philadelphia PA
2. Jacksonville FL
3. Columbus OH
4. Indianapolis IN
5. Charlotte NC
6. Nashville TN
7. Washington DC
8. Boston MA
9. Detroit MI
10. Louisville, KY
11. Memphis TN

3
1. Alabama
2. Arizona
3. Arkansas
4. Georgia
5. Florida
6. Mississippi
7. Missouri
8. Nebraska
9. Oklahoma
10. South Dakota
11. Texas

4
1. Wisconsin
2. Texas
3. Oregon
4. North Carolina
5. Montana
6. Mississippi
7. Michigan
8. Minnesota
9. Maryland
10. Kansas
11. Indiana
12. Alabama

5
1. New York, NY
2. Denver, CO
3. Washington DC
4. San Marino, CA
5. Houston, TX
6. Chicago IL
7. Bentonville AR
8. Chantilly, VA
9. Los Angeles CA
10. Richmond VA
11. Boston, MA

6
1. Mississippi
2. Louisiana
3. New Mexico
4. West Virginia
5. Kentucky
6. Arkansas
7. Alabama
8. Oklahoma
9. South Carolina
10. Tennessee
11. Georgia
12. Texas
13. Arizona

7
1. Princeton
2. Massachusetts Institue of Technology (M.I.T.)
3. Harvard
4. Stanford
5. Yale
6. University of Chicago
7. Johns Hopkins
8. University of Pennsylvania
9. California Institute of Technology (CalTech)
10. Duke
11. Northwestern

8
1. Minnesota
2. Wisconsin
3. Iowa
4. Illinois
5. Missouri
6. Kentucky
7. Tennessee
8. Arkansas
9. Mississippi
10. Louisiana

9
1. Michelle Obama
2. Hillary Clinton
3. Laura Bush
4. Mother Theresa
5. Barbara Bush
6. Margaret Thatcher
7. Nancy Reagan
8. Rosalynn Carter
9. Betty Ford
10. Golda Meir

10
1. Houston, FL
2. Miami, FL
3. Tampa, FL
4. New Orleans, LA
5. Corpus Christi, TX
6. Orlando, FL
7. St Petersburg, FL
8. Baton Rouge, LA
9. Tallahassee, FL
10. Cape Coral, FL
11. Mobile, AL
12. Brownsville, TX
13. Pembroke Pines, FL
14. Pasadena TX
15. McAllen, TX

Winter Olympics K♠

A	Choose a Question

2	7 women and 7 men have won a Gold Medal in Singles Figure skating representing the United States. Name them

3	The USA team has competed in all Winter Olympic games, without skipping or reorganizing as a new nation. Only 11 other countries can also claim this. Name them

4	In figure skating, there are 7 basic types of Jumps, and 3 basic forms of spins that are acceptable for required elements at the Olympics. Name them

5	Ice Hockey is dominated by a small number of great teams at the Olympics. Only 7 countries have ever won Gold, and only 10 have ever even played in a medal qualifying final. Name these 10 Countries

6	Italy is 11th All-Time in total Winter Olympic Medals with 138 Name the 10 Countries that have more than Italy.

7	At the Winter Olympics, there are 10 individual events that do not require one to wear skates or skis on their feet. Name them.

8	23 Women have won Singles Figure Skating Gold Medals representing 12 different Countries. Name the 12 Countries

9	The upcoming 2026 Winter Olympics will be held for the 3rd time in Italy, aside from this country, 12 other countries have hosted the Winter games. Name them

10	The next Winter Olympics will be held in 2026 in Cortina-Milan. The 1980 Olympics were held in Lake Placid, Name any of the 11 Winter Olympic cities that hosted in between

Winter Olympics K♠

2
1. Space HolderTenley Albright
2. Carol Heiss
3. Peggy Fleming
4. Dorothy Hamil
5. Kristi Yamaguchi
6. Tara Lipinski
7. Sarah Hughes
8. Dick Button
9. Hayes Alan Jenkins
10. David Jenkins
11. Scott Hamilton
12. Brian Boitano
13. Evan Lysacek
14. Nathan Chen

3
1. Hungary
2. Poland
3. Great Britain
4. France
5. Italy
6. Finland
7. Switzerland
8. Sweden
9. Austria
10. Canada
11. Norway
12. Space Holder

4
1. Toe (Jump)
2. Salchow (Jump)
3. Loop (Jump)
4. Flip (Jump)
5. Axel (Jump)
6. Lutz (Jump)
7. Euler (Jump)
8. Standing (Spin)
9. Sit (Spin)
10. Camel (Spin)

5
1. Canada
2. USA
3. Sweden
4. Great Britain
5. Czechoslovakia
6. Soviet Union/Russia
7. Finland
8. Germany
9. Belarus
10. Poland

6
1. Norway
2. Germany (inc East & West)
3. USA
4. Russia/Soviet Union
5. Canada
6. Austria
7. Sweden
8. Switzerland
9. Netherlands
10. Finland

7
1. SBobsleigh
2. Monobob
3. Luge
4. Skeleton
5. Curling
6. Snowboard Cross
7. Aerialls (Snowboard)
8. Half Pipe (Snowboard)
9. Parallel (Snowboard)
10. Big Air (Snowboard)

8
1. USA
2. Germany (East)
3. Norway
4. Russia
5. Great Britain
6. Austria
7. Sweden
8. Canada
9. Netherlands
10. Ukraine
11. Japan
12. So Korea

9
1. China
2. So Korea
3. Russia
4. Canada
5. USA
6. Japan
7. Norway
8. France
9. Yugoslavia
10. Austria
11. Switzerland
12. Germany

10
1. Beijing (China)
2. Pyongyang (So Korea)
3. Sochi (Russia)
4. Vancouver (Canada)
5. Turin (Italy)
6. Salt Lake City (USA)
7. Nagano (Japan)
8. Lillihammer (Norway)
9. Albertvillw (France)
10. Calgary (Canada)
11. Sarajevo (Yugoslavia)

TRIAL BY TRIVIA

This is a unique new trivia game based on the principles of fun, knowledge, choice, constant involvement, the game never being over until it's over, & the fecund hand of fate. The game play is simple: A question is drawn that has between 10 and 20 possible answers. Each team alternates giving an answer they believe is correct without duplicating previous answers. The winner of each question is awarded a draw or draws. You can win the round in either of three ways: (1) you give the 9th answer and it is correct, (2) You give a correct answer that is challenged, or (3) you challenge an answer that is incorrect. At the end of the game, the values of cards won are revealed and a winner is crowned. The game runs for 12 rounds (the final six being bonus rounds) and the game should run between 30-45 minutes.

The game is divided into three parts: **The Setup** (choosing categories), **the Trials** (head-to-head question answering phase), and **the Verdict** (calculating the winner).

THE SETUP

Starting with a freshly shuffled deck of cards, teams alternate drawing a card. Each card corresponds to a particular category. These categories are recorded on a piece of paper and this creates the field of play for a particular game. This is done until 10 categories are chosen. During this portion, each team is allowed 2 peremptory challenges, basically allowing a team to remove a drawn category because one doesn't like it, creating an additional draw. One can only challenge a category before it's agreed to and written down (e.g. you can't remove the 3rd category, during the 8th category draw, but only during the categories consideration phase). After 10 categories are randomly chosen, each team selects 2 categories each, to get the category pool up to 14.

Once the 14 categories of play are determined, the cards are reshuffled and each team is dealt 2 random starting cards.

THE TRIAL

Play begins here. One team looks at the list of categories and offers a choice of 2 categories to the team whose turn it is. That team then draws a card that corresponds to a question on the category page. If an Ace is drawn, the questioning team can choose any question on the page.   If a Queen or King is drawn, a bonus card is pulled from the deck, and the winner of the round will get this additional card, while a new card is drawn to determine the question.   If the Jack is drawn, the category is switched to the rejected category and a card is drawn to determine the question asked on the new page.

There are 2 ways you can lose your turn during this phase. First, if two consecutive Jacks are drawn, the first changing the question, then another. Second, if three bonus cards are drawn. One bonus card is fine, two is fine, but a third ends the turn with the bonus cards being placed in the discard pile. If you lose a turn, the round just ends without cards awarded and two categories are offered to the other team.

After a question is determined, it is asked. Normally, because these questions are challenging, 1 or 2 minutes should be allotted so teams can discuss and make notes in preparation. The first team answers, the other team responds by either accepting the answer (do this by giving a new answer for consideration), challenging the answer, passing, or vetoing the question. Answers are traded back and forth until the 9th answer is given without challenge or a challenge is made. When a question is played through, strikethrough the category name of the category list so it will not be offered again. After 6 categories are completed, rounds 7 thru 12 start with one bonus card, so the round is playing for two cards. The game runs 12 rounds, two categories will not be completed and may not even be played.

WINNING THE ROUND - The team wins the round if any of these things happen:
> ➢ The team is challenged on an answer and the answer is deemed correct (acceptable).
> ➢ The team challenges an answer and that answer is deemed incorrect (unacceptable).
> ➢ The team answers the 9th and Final Answer and is unchallenged as to correctness.

The winner of the round earns a draw and any applicable bonus cards. That draw is from the deck, except for when a team is falsely challenged, then the draw is from the challenging team's group of cards.

THE VETO - At the beginning of the round before your team gives its first answer, a team can remove the question, ending play.   At the beginning of the game, either team can veto, but once a team vetoes a question, they may not do so again until every team has vetoed once (and so forth, you can't use your 4th veto until all teams have vetoed thrice). This sets the game back to the category stage, with the same team who offered 2 categories offering 2 categories again (the vetoed question's category may not be offered).

THE PASS - You can pass on an answer. Each team starts the game with one "Free" pass, but every pass after will come with the cost of discarding a card. A "passed" answer counts as an unchallengeable correct answer.

THE CHALLENGE - If you believe the answer given is wrong, you can challenge that answer. If you are right you win the round and the appropriate draws. However if you are wrong, the winning team draws a card from your cards rather than the card stack as a penalty for an incorrect challenge. The team with the incorrect challenge must offer 5 cards to be chosen from (if you have less than 5 all cards must be offered). This allows the protection of as many as 3 cards in the end game.

THE DECK DRAW - If you draw a club from the deck, you can show the card and receive an additional draw (this additional draw cannot result in additional draws even if a club)

During the course of the game the maximum number of cards you can have at the end of a turn is 8. Excess cards must be discarded. You are allowed to draw all cards won in a round before discarding (e.g. if you have 7 cards, and win 3 cards, you can temporarily be at 10, but must discard 2 before a new question is asked or scores can be tabulated.)

THE VERDICT

After 12 rounds are played, both teams gather their cards and put together the best possible 5 card poker hand. These are revealed and the team with the winning poker hand is awarded 10.5 points (the .5 avoids ties). Next the team that lost the poker hand counts their cards' value. A Club is worth 1 point, A Diamond 2, a Heart 3, and a Spade 4. Then the poker winner counts adding in the 10.5 point bonus. The team with the most points wins.

OTHER CONSIDERATIONS

SCORING	VALUE
CLUBS	1
DIAMONDS	2
HEARTS	3
SPADES	4
BEST POKER HAND	10.5 (TO ONE TEAM)

- ➢ Many, if not most, cards will be won via the challenge, as there is a finite number of "right" answers and an infinite number of "wrong" ones. These cards are earned justly because you can only win a challenge if your team has provided the last accepted as correct answer.
- ➢ There is no timer provided. This is partly a cost saving decision, but mostly a philosophical one.   The best part of trivia is the process of coming up with your best answer, especially when it's correct. If there's meaningful discussion, let it flow, using what we call the "popcorn" rule.   You microwave popcorn until you stop hearing the pops. Similarly, you allow discussion to go til the "pops" stop (or are few and far between). If a team seems to be taking advantage of this rule, most phones come with a stopwatch function and it can be implemented.
- ➢ Duplicate answers are going to come up. It's the duty of the team to point out this duplication when it's offered, to allow the team to offer a new answer. If it isn't called out, it can be accepted as a right answer (wrong answers can be considered right, so why not?)
- ➢ There is another option on your turn if you don't know the answer: You can and should bluff, give an answer that may be wrong but sounds good enough the other team won't know or risk challenging. The cost of a failed challenge becomes more costly as the game progresses.

- ➢ The Questions are on odd numbered pages; the answers are on the reverse side of that page (even numbers).
- ➢ The team that is asked the question first is consider the team up because they will be the team up to give the 9th and final answer
- ➢ A question is considered complete once the answers are checked or the final (9th) answer is given. If a category is accidentally struck through improperly simply rewrite the category so it can be chosen again. One great thing about this game is by limiting the checking of answers many questions can be replayed because one doesn't know if answers heard are actually correct.
- ➢ If you run low on cards to draw from (10 cards or less), shuffle the discards into the draw pile
- ➢ If 9 answers proves too difficult, you may consider playing to a smaller number (Maybe 7 or 5 for a more approachable game)

THREE PERSON GAME

The game is intended for two teams, but in the event you have three individual players (or a large enough crowd for three teams), some rules must be altered.

- ➢ In the setup phase, 10 categories are drawn randomly, with each of the three getting to choose 2 categories, creating 16 potential categories
- ➢ 14 rounds are played instead of 12, with the bonus rounds being round 8-14
- ➢ During the Trial play, the answers are still back and forth with the team up answering against the two teams who need to agree on one answer.
- ➢ A challenge must be agreed to by both other teams.
- ➢ If a joint challenge is victorious both teams draw an equal number of cards (e.g. if 2 bonus cards are in play, normally allowing a 3 card pickup, a single card from the deck is added and each team gets 2 cards each).
- ➢ if a joint challenge is incorrect the team gets to choose which team to draw its penalty card from.

CATEGORIES

The categories have been selected to update the changes in the culture (more questions about food, about technology, and reflective of the boom in the entertainment industry), while paying due respect to traditional trivia categories. The category titles should give you a general, yet imperfect understanding of the kinds of questions that may come. A few topics particular to this game are of note:

MISCELLANEOUS

The categories with name that more or less mean miscellaneous (**Amalgam**, **HodgePodge**, **Pastiche**, or **Sundries**) are reserved for questions that either don't fit a category, aren't deep enough a topic to have 9 questions, or extra questions from other categories that we liked. It's a wild card situation and you really don't know what you'll get.

<u>PAIRED QUESTIONS</u>

A playable question has 10 or more answers. **Paired Questions** (or **Questions Paired**) takes two questions in related or unrelated fields with between 4 and 7 answers and combines them to make one qualifying question. You may answer either side of the question. It's a good mental challenge to try to keep separate concepts in your mind simultaneously.

<u>VS. A.I.</u>

This idea came up with the rise of A.I. in 2023. It actually inspired a companion game *BR A.I. NS*, which is also available. In these questions, we ask an A.I. to give us 10 to 15 answers to a question, and teams try to answer what the A.I. says.   The A.I. is mostly correct, but not 100%. The 3 categories are classified by what the answer will be in the form of, either a **person**, a **place**, or a **thing.** This also gives the opportunity for questions with more subjective answers.

→HELP THE CREATORS

First, thank you so much for buying or renting or even just playing our game. We put forth significant effort in hopes that it will result in your enjoyment.

Second, Please review this game as you see it on Amazon.   Hopefully it will be favorable.

Third, tell people about this book/game. Easiest way is to play it with others

Fourth, if in playing you find you want to add a twist to the rules, give it a shot. If it seems to enhance the game email us and let us know about it (urbanbaboon@gmail.com)

Fifth, we are looking for someone to adapt this game (and the next one) into an app format. If you have those skills, email us and express your interest. (urbanbaboon@gmail.com)

Finally, Thank you once again for sharing your time in this manner.

TRIVIA MAN says "Good Bye"

www.ingramcontent.com/pod-product-compliance
Lightning Source LLC
Chambersburg PA
CBHW080931260726
48661CB00010B/3877